E
Guidelin

How do we know right from wrong? How can we judge the behaviour of other people?

Ethics are the rules and guidelines that we use to make judgements of right and wrong. Psychologists have to consider ethical issues because they deal with people and study their behaviour on a daily basis. The study of ethics is one of the more difficult areas of psychology because there are no clear answers. That might well make it one of the more interesting areas for you, or one of the most frustrating. In this book we offer you the opportunity to develop and express your own opinion in relation to ethics in psychology.

The book explains some key ethical issues and reviews the various ethical principles and guidelines developed by professional bodies. The problems relating to different kinds of research are discussed, as well as the special case of socially sensitive research. Finally the question of the use of animals in research is examined – is it useful and is it right to use non-human animals in psychological research?

Philip Banyard is Associate Senior Lecturer in Psychology at Nottingham Trent University.

Cara Flanagan is a widely published freelance author and experienced senior examiner.

Routledge Modular Psychology

Series editors: Cara Flanagan is a freelance academic author and an experienced teacher and examiner for AS and A2 level psychology. Philip Banyard is Associate Senior Lecturer in Psychology at Nottingham Trent University and has 20 years experience as a Chief Examiner for GCSE and A level Psychology.

The *Routledge Modular Psychology* series is a completely new approach to introductory level psychology, tailor-made to the new modular style of teaching. Each short book covers a topic in more detail than any large textbook can, allowing teacher and student to select material exactly to suit any particular course or project.

The books have been written especially for those students new to higher level study, whether at school, college or university. They include specially designed features to help with technique, such as a model essay at an average level with an examiner's comments to show how extra marks can be gained. The authors are all examiners and teachers at the introductory level.

The *Routledge Modular Psychology* texts are all user friendly and accessible and use the following features:

- practice essays with specialist commentary to show how to achieve a higher grade
- chapter summaries to assist with revision
- progress and review exercises
- glossary of key terms
- summaries of key research
- further reading to stimulate ongoing study and research
- cross-referencing to other books in the series

For more details on our AS, A2 and *Routledge Modular Psychology* publications visit our website at www.a-levelpsychology.co.uk

Also available in this series (titles listed by syllabus section):

ATYPICAL DEVELOPMENT AND ABNORMAL BEHAVIOUR
Classification and Diagnosis of Psychological Abnormality
Susan Cave

Psychopathology
John D. Stirling and Jonathan S.E. Hellewell

Therapeutic Approaches in Psychology
Susan Cave

BIO-PSYCHOLOGY
Awareness: Biorhythms, sleep and dreaming
Evie Bentley

Cortical Functions
John Stirling

Motivation and Emotion
Phil Gorman

The Physiological Basis of Behaviour: Neural and hormonal processes
Kevin Silber

COGNITIVE PSYCHOLOGY
Attention and Pattern Recognition
Nick Lund

Language and Thought
Nick Lund

Memory and Forgetting
John Henderson

Perception: Theory, development and organisation
Paul Rookes and Jane Willson

DEVELOPMENTAL PSYCHOLOGY
Early Socialisation: Sociability and attachment
Cara Flanagan

Social and Personality Development
Tina Abbott

PERSPECTIVES AND RESEARCH
Cognitive Development
Lisa Oakley

Controversies in Psychology
Philip Banyard

Debates in Psychology
Andy Bell

Ethical Issues and Guidelines in Psychology
Cara Flanagan and Philip Banyard (forthcoming)

Introducing Research and Data in Psychology: A guide to methods and analysis
Ann Searle

Theoretical Approaches in Psychology
Matt Jarvis

SOCIAL PSYCHOLOGY
Interpersonal Relationships
Diana Dwyer

Pro-Social and Anti-Social Behaviour
David Clarke

Social Cognition
Donald C. Pennington

Social Influences
Kevin Wren

COMPARATIVE PSYCHOLOGY
Animal Cognition
Nick Lund

Determinants of Animal Behaviour
Jo-Anne Cartwright

Evolutionary Explanations of Human Behaviour
John Cartwright

OTHER TITLES
Health Psychology
Anthony Curtis

Psychology and Crime
David Putwain and Aidan Sammons

Psychology and Education
Susan Bentham

Psychology and Work
Christine Hodson

Sport Psychology
Matt Jarvis

STUDY GUIDE
Exam Success in AQA-A Psychology
Paul Humphreys (forthcoming)

Ethical Issues and Guidelines in Psychology

Philip Banyard and Cara Flanagan

UNIVERSITY OF WINCHESTER
LIBRARY

Routledge
Taylor & Francis Group

LONDON AND NEW YORK

First published 2005
by Routledge
27 Church Road, Hove, East Sussex BN3 2FA

Simultaneously published in the USA and Canada
by Routledge
270 Madison Avenue, New York NY 10016

Routledge is an imprint of the Taylor & Francis Group

© 2005 Routledge

Typeset in Times and Frutiger by Keystroke,
Jacaranda Lodge, Wolverhampton
Printed and bound in Great Britain by
TJ International Ltd, Padstow, Cornwall
Paperback cover design by Anú Design

This publication has been produced with paper manufactured to strict
environmental standards and with pulp derived from sustainable forests.

British Library Cataloguing in Publication Data
A catalogue record for this book is available from the British Library

Library of Congress Cataloging-in-Publication Data
A catalog record for this book has been applied for

ISBN 0-415-26880-X (hbk)
ISBN 0-415-26881-8 (pbk)

Contents

Illustrations

Acknowledgements

Phil Banyard would like to acknowledge the support he gets from his colleagues, family, friends and students in his work. In particular he would like to thank them for humouring his irrational rants against the world and everything. He would also like to thank the following for providing absurd and pointless behaviour for him to rant at: media psychologists, weather forecasters, the management of Heathrow airport and Nottingham Forest football club. He would also like to acknowledge the support of his co-author Cara for her patience and tolerance. Maybe he will develop those qualities himself one day.

Cara Flanagan would like to thank her partner and children for their willingness to remain friendly despite the long hours she spends conversing with her computer. She also thanks her co-author for his special gift with words and ideas.

The authors would also like to thank Matt Jarvis and Andy Bell for their very useful comments on the first draft of this book, and the team at Routledge for their forbearance. Finally we would like to thank Mike Cardwell for giving us this opportunity.

Acknowledgement

1

Introduction

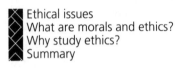

Ethical issues
What are morals and ethics?
Why study ethics?
Summary

In this chapter we will look at what we mean by ethics. We will consider an array of terms such as morals, ethical issues, ethical guidelines, human rights, ethical relativism and utilitarianism, to name but a few. These can be easily confused by the reader (and by authors to be fair) but we will try and work our way through as best we can in order to better understand how psychologists develop their ideas of right and wrong and how we end up with the ethical codes that guide our behaviour. First though, look below at two examples of scientific studies that have raised some serious ethical concerns.

The Tuskegee experiment

In 1932 the US Public Health Service began an investigation into the long-term effects of untreated syphilis. The researchers promised 400 men free treatment for 'bad blood' – a polite word for syphilis which was rife at that time in the state of Alabama. The Tuskegee experiment lasted for 40 years and was finally exposed by a journalist, Jean Heller, in 1972. It emerged that there had never been any intention to treat the men suffering from syphilis. The aim of the study was to observe the natural course of the disease. Untreated syphilis can lead to mental illness and early death, and it is estimated that between 28 and 100 of the men died as a result of their syphilis. It is also likely that many of the men passed on the disease to partners and children. It may not surprise you to know that the men were all black and all poor. These men were duped. They were offered incentives to participate: free physical examinations, free rides to and from the clinics, hot meals on examination days, free treatment for minor ailments, and a guarantee that a sum of $50 would be paid when they died. They were given a medication but it was just something for the common cold (Jones 1993).

Why did the researchers do it? Perhaps they felt it was important to record objective data about syphilis and the value of this research should justify the liberties they took. With retrospect this has been called 'America's dirty little secret' as well as 'America's Nuremberg'. The reference to Nuremberg is that this was where Nazi war criminals were tried, some for their participation in medical experiments without the consent of patients (we will discuss this shortly).

What happened to the men from Tuskegee, and their survivors? After the study was publicised in 1972 the participants sued the US government and an out-of-court settlement was made to the men or their surviving relatives. In 1997 President Clinton gave an official apology.

One important outcome of the Tuskegee experiment, and some other medical experiments, has been the introduction of stricter ethical standards. It made officials aware of the potential for harm in scientific research and of researchers' responsibilities.

HM

The case study of HM appears in many introductory psychology texts. It concerns a man who lost the ability to remember information after a brain operation. He is very famous in psychology and 'he has probably had more words written about him than any other case in neurological or psychological history' (Ogden and Corkin 1991: 195).

HM is always given initials to protect his identity, though that might seem ironic after you read about what the psychologists did to him. He was born in 1926 and had a head injury at the age of 7 that started a lifetime of epileptic seizures. These seizures got worse over the years and in his mid twenties he was having uncontrolled grand mal attacks (health-threatening seizures). It was proposed to attempt a brain operation to a cure the epilepsy and a surgeon called Scoville performed the first 'bilateral medial temporal lobe resection' in the world (an operation that involved cutting out that part of HM's brain). On the good side, HM survived the operation and his epilepsy was now less damaging, but on the very big downside he had profound retrograde and anterograde amnesia. More precisely, he had lost much of his memory for the ten years prior to the operation (retrograde amnesia), and even more damagingly, he had lost the ability to store new information (anterograde amnesia). He had a memory span of just a few minutes, so he was effectively waking up every few minutes not knowing where he was or who he was talking to:

> [The first psychological examination] was performed on April 26, 1955. The memory defect was immediately apparent. The patient gave the date as March, 1953, and his age as 27. Just before coming into the examining room he had been talking to Dr. Karl Pribram, yet he had no recollection of this at all and denied that anyone had spoken to him. In conversation, he reverted constantly to boyhood events and seemed scarcely to realize that he had had an operation. (Scoville and Milner 1957: 16)

This was clearly a disaster for HM though he probably never understood that because he could never learn what happened to him, or if he did he would forget it within a couple of minutes. This was a tragedy for HM, but an opportunity for psychologists who became aware of the case. They queued up to study HM's memory, assessing it with all kinds of tests and checking out a wide range of hypotheses concerning the theoretical distinctions between long-term and short-term memory, and between explicit and implicit memory. They used all sorts of stimuli including electric shocks and white noise (for a review see Corkin 1984, or Parkin 1996). One of 'the most striking characteristics is that he rarely complains about anything . . . is always agreeable and co-operative to the point that if . . . asked to sit in a particular place he will do so indefinitely' (Corkin 1984: 251). In other words he was an ideal subject of study.

The tests continued for 40 years until HM was in his late sixties and his mental faculties were starting to show a general deterioration. One of the psychologists wrote of the major contribution this work had made to our understanding of memory and commented 'the fact that he has no conscious memory of this work does not in any way detract from the debt we owe him' (Ogden and Corkin 1991). The story of HM is commonly presented without comment in psychology books, but ask yourself this: how did HM give consent for the 40 years of constant experimentation? He did not know what was being done to him or even who was doing it. Is this ground-breaking science or cruel exploitation of a man whose life has been ruined by experimental brain surgery? Are the benefits of this research outweighed by the costs? An interesting and disturbing footnote is that the tragedy of HM is often presented as a unique case but the operation was carried out on a number of people with psychiatric conditions who also experienced memory loss (Scoville and Milner 1957). This raises a further ethical issue because it is possible to make a mistake and carry out an operation with unforeseen consequences but after the first one, the consequences must have been expected.

Ethical issues

These two cases highlight some central **ethical issues**: First there is the issue of **informed consent**, which refers to the idea that any participant in an experiment should be informed about what the research entails and asked formally to consent to take part. This basic human right was first recognised by the Nuremberg trials. During World War II (1939–45) Nazi doctors conducted various experiments on prisoners. For example, the doctors tested their reactions to fatal diseases such as typhoid, and to extreme temperatures by immersing them in freezing water to see how long it would take for them to die. After the war a ten-point code (Nuremberg Code) was produced which has formed the basis for many contemporary ethical codes in both medical and behavioural research (Box 1.1).

The second issue raised by the two studies above is the one of *costs versus benefits*. All researchers believe that their research offers potential benefits and they recognise that there are certain costs. The difficulty is in assessing the costs and benefits, and then deciding whether the research is justified. In the case of medical research, it is

Box 1.1 The Nuremberg Code (1946)

1. The voluntary consent of the human subject is absolutely essential.
2. The experiment should yield fruitful results for the good of society, that cannot be obtained by other means.
3. The experiment should be based on previous research so that the anticipated results can justify the research.
4. All unnecessary physical and mental suffering should be avoided.
5. No experiment should be conducted where there is reason to believe that death or disabling injury may be the result.
6. The degree of risk should also be less than the potential humanitarian importance of the research.
7. Adequate precautions should be in place to protect the subjects against any possible injury.
8. Experiments should only be conducted by qualified persons.
9. The human subject should always be at liberty to end the experiment.
10. The scientist in charge should be prepared to terminate any experiment if there is probable cause to believe that continuation is likely to result in injury or death.

Source: Adapted from Katz (1972).

Progress exercise

Consider the case of HM described on pages 2–4. Which of the above points were violated in the research conducted with HM?

easier to assess benefits but, as we will see, this is much harder in the behavioural sciences because the potential benefits to others are less easy to define. These issues are explored again in Chapter 2.

The third issue raised by these studies is the modern expectation that scientists treat all people with respect and take all reasonable steps to *protect their welfare*. If we see some people as less important than others, then it might seem OK to experiment on them so that the more important people can have some benefit. The syphilis study and the wartime experimentation were both carried out on people who were regarded as less worthy of respect. We have to acknowledge that even today we do not grant all people equal respect. For example, in this country we are happy to buy branded sports clothing that is made under working conditions in the developing world which would not be tolerated in our own country. This can only be based on the underlying belief that the welfare of Indonesian children is not as important as British children.

What are morals and ethics?

It all starts with morals, which are rules to guide our behaviour. They are based on a number of socially agreed principles which are used to develop clear and logical guidelines to direct behaviour. They also contain ideas about what is good and what is desirable in human behaviour. Ethics are a moral framework that is applied to a narrow group of people such as doctors, or maybe a particular religion or psychologists (Box 1.2).

Box 1.2   Morals and ethics

There are a number of terms that we ought to consider and try and make sense of. They do not have clear-cut definitions so the terms we decide to use might be a little different from some other books.

We start with MORALS which are *'concerned with or relating to human behaviour, especially the distinction between good and bad or right and wrong behaviour'* (Source: *The Collins English Dictionary* © 2000 Harper-Collins Publishers).

From morals we move on to ETHICS. It is important to distinguish between PRIVATE MORALS (which may vary from person to person) and PROFESSIONAL ETHICS. The latter are the generally agreed standards of behaviour or guidelines for behaviour.

This term ETHICS has two meanings: one is *'a social, religious, or civil code of behaviour considered correct, especially that of a particular group, profession, or individual'*; the other *is 'the philosophical study of the moral value of human conduct and of the rules and principles that ought to govern*

---

it; moral philosophy' (both definitions from *The Collins English Dictionary* © 2000 HarperCollins Publishers). If you took an ethics course at university you would probably be most concerned with the second definition, but for the basis of a psychology course we are mostly concerned with the first definition: the code of conduct that psychologists use to regulate their professional behaviour.

When we look at ethics for psychologists we might start off by stating some PRINCIPLES which form the basis for our ethical judgements. From these principles we might develop some GUIDELINES for behaviour or maybe a CODE OF CONDUCT. When we try to use these ethical principles and guidelines we sometimes have to wrestle with some ethical ISSUES. An issue is something which arises because of a conflict. In the case of psychological research it is usually a conflict between the requirements of meaningful research (e.g. deception) and the rights of participants (e.g. to be treated honestly).

The distinctions between all these terms are not clear cut. One person's issue might be another person's principle: for example, informed consent can be seen as an issue (should all participants have the right of informed consent) or a principle (informed consent is a prerequisite of any research). The various organisations that develop codes of ethics use the terms in different ways: for example, the American Psychological Association refers to an Ethics Code whereas the British Psychological Society refers to 'Ethical principles for conducting research with human participants' and 'Guidelines for psychologists working with animals'.

The labels are not that important but the debate is. It is all about right and wrong, good and bad, and the way we choose to conduct our lives. What can be more important than that?

The ethics of a behaviour can be judged using four categories (Daeg de Mott 2001): *consequences, actions, character* and *motive*. When we look at *consequences*, we judge whether a behaviour is right or wrong by looking at the result of the behaviour. If it leads to a result that brings about an improvement for someone's life, we might think it is a good thing. When we look at the *actions*, however, we look at the act itself, and consider what the person is doing. The category of *character* is concerned with whether the person is a good (or virtuous) person who is generally ethical. When we look at *motives*, we are concerned with the intentions of the person carrying out the behaviour, and we consider whether they were trying to do something good.

Nothing is clear-cut in the study of ethics and these categories sometimes give us different assessments. The puzzle is to decide whether *you* think the behaviour is ethical or not. Look at the following two examples and see what you think.

Example one: therapy

> *Rapoff (1980) used an ammonia spray to punish a deaf-blind five year old boy who was engaging in serious self-injurious behaviour (self-mutilation), and in so doing reduced the amount of self-harmful behaviour.*

This sounds a shocking thing to do and many of you will immediately decide that this treatment is unethical but we are going to argue the opposite. The *consequence* of this action, if it is successful, is that the boy will have a better quality of life. The *act* does not look to be a good thing, but we might well judge the *motives* of the therapist to be sound because they want to help the child. Depending on what we believe about therapists in general, or what we know about Rapoff in particular, we can make an assessment of *character* and decide whether we trust them to do the right thing. Considering that there are no easy solutions when dealing with very challenging children and that this solution at least avoids the use of medication, one might be inclined to judge this as an ethical treatment. Feel free to disagree.

Example two: war

> *Your government decides to go to war. At the time of writing the most recent military engagement by the UK's forces has been in Iraq, and a debate is still raging about whether we should have gone in. Everyone (well nearly everyone) is against war in principle, but the issue is whether in practice this war was necessary or right.*

The same four categories structure the debate. The *consequence* of the action is used as an ethical justification for the war. The removal of a murderous government is generally seen as a good thing, though history will be the final judge of this. The *act* of war itself is generally seen as bad because of the chaos, loss of life and general destruction that it brings. The bitterest part of the argument concerns character and motives. The US and UK governments argue that their *motive* for action was honourable and humanitarian, but some see their actions as being led by commercial interests such as control of oil. The key issue for many in the UK is their assessment of Prime Minister Tony Blair's *character*. If you largely trust him to do the right thing then you might well go along, however reluctantly, with the decision to go to war with Iraq.

Think of an example of something that has been publicly debated as right or wrong, for example, using capital punishment for people who kill other people. Or you might consider a more psychological dilemma such as whether it is right to harm adult participants in an experiment who have agreed to be distressed (in the same way that *Big Brother* contestants have agreed to be humiliated).

Is it ever morally right to kill or harm another person?
If you think it is, give some examples of killing or harming that might be justified.

Is it right to use the death penalty if one person kills another?
If you think it is, give some examples of when it would be justified and also some when it would not: for example, if a police officer kills someone in the line of duty; or an ambulance driver kills someone in a road accident, or a drunk driver kills someone in a road accident.

Use the four categories of *consequences, actions, character* and *motive* to decide on the ethics of these behaviours.

Progress exercise

Absolute and relative morals

Broadly speaking, there are two approaches to solving moral dilemmas. Either you take the view that morals are **absolute** or that they are **relative**. The absolute view is that some things are simply right or wrong. The absolutist position corresponds to common traditional views of morality, particularly of a religious kind which might be called the 'Ten Commandments' idea of morality; for example, 'thou shalt not steal'.

Relativists, on the other hand, believe that all morals are dependent on context so, for example, they argue that there are situations where stealing is acceptable. The intrinsic 'wrongness' of an act may be overridden by other considerations. For example, it might be acceptable for a father to steal food because his children are starving.

As ever in these debates between two extreme positions, the common response is somewhere between the two. Most people who tend towards absolutism will allow for special circumstances and bend the rules on special occasions, while those who favour relativism are still likely to admit to some universal standards that form a 'bottom line' of behaviour.

It is the generally held view in Britain that we should respect other people's property and not steal, but despite expressing morals near the *absolutist* end, many people behave in a *relativist* way. For example, most people will not go into a local Virgin Megastore and steal CDs, and the reason they may give for this is that they do not think it is right to steal. They might then go home, however, and log onto Kazaa, or another peer-to-peer music sharing service, and download music to burn onto their own CDs. This is theft just as much as swiping CDs from the Virgin Megastore. The reasons given for this theft might be that 'the record companies charge too much for music and are exploiting us' which would suggest high moral principles, or 'I won't get caught', which suggests that morals are determined by reward and punishment (*all right, I confess, but I won't do it again – ed*).

It is very difficult to keep to an absolutist line even though we try (Box 1.3). As a result it is very easy to call someone a hypocrite because they appear to be doing something that they do not believe in. The above is a good example of this.

Rights and values

Many people claim the 'right to work' or the 'right to good health care' or the 'right to have children', but what are 'rights'? This is more controversial than you might think. It depends, in part, on where you think rights come from. According to Fukuyama (2001) there are three lines of argument about the source of rights: divine rights, natural rights, or rights from custom and practice. In other words rights can come from *God*, or from *nature* or from *human beings*.

Box 1.3 Moral perspectives

Along the continuum of absolute–relative there are a number of moral perspectives. The *deontological* perspective (e.g. Immanuel Kant) holds that there are things that are intrinsically right or wrong but there may be exceptional circumstances which can override this position. It is largely an absolutist position. Deontological ethics emphasise universal imperatives like moral laws, duties, obligations, prohibitions, and so on (sometimes this is also called 'imperativism').

Moral relativism is the view that moral judgements are true or false only relative to a particular context. So if I say that eating people is wrong, while you say it is right, we may both be speaking the truth. For cannibalism may be wrong in my context and right in yours (for example, as part of a cultural ritual or consider the case of the survivors of the plane wreck in the Andes dramatized in the film *Alive*, where they decide to eat those passengers who had died). Morals are relative to historical or cultural contexts.

Utilitarianism (e.g. John Stuart Mill) says simply that an action is right or wrong depending upon its consequences, such as its effects on society (sometimes this is also called *consequentialism*). An act is good or moral if it produces the greatest well-being for everyone affected by it. The *cost-benefit* approach taken by most ethical codes is based on this idea of consequences or utility.

First let us consider divine rights. In a religious society, the rights are seen to come from the God of that society, and are commonly written in a holy book and interpreted by religious scholars. If we do not believe in divine rights we might argue that rights come from nature, and that we should look at human nature to see what people are capable of and what can be viewed as right or wrong.

Thus we come to the second of Fukuyama's rights, natural rights. The issue here is to describe human nature and to say what parts of our behaviour are inevitable and what parts are created by the world we live in. This is clearly tricky because the world we live in has been created by ourselves and so we can end up in a circular argument: society affects the behaviour of people but people affect the structure of society. It is also not a popular argument with liberals and guardianistas[1] because the study of human nature can give us an uncomfortable picture of ourselves as selfish, murderous and xenophobic.

The third possible source of human rights is human beings them-selves – rights from custom and practice. William F. Schulz (2000) the executive director of Amnesty International, argues that human rights should not be concerned with human nature but with the things 'human beings possess or can claim'; in other words, human rights are anything we agree them to be. An example of this approach is the United Nations Universal Declaration of Human Rights (1948, see Box 1.4). This was a political document written to keep both the United States and the Soviet Union happy at a time when their Cold War[2] conflict was just beginning. If you read through it you will find some absurdities such as article 24 which states we have a right to 'periodic holidays with pay'. In a world where less than half the population have paid employment, this is nonsense. And what about article 19, the right to freedom of expression? This sounds fine and dandy but in this country we are (rightly, we believe) forbidden from freely expressing racist views. In this case, rights are not absolute principles.

Since 1948 people have been enthusiastically adding rights to the list. It has become a 'wish list' that has no end. Some of the new 'rights' highlight the difficulty of this process. If you consider the idea of 'animal rights', then you can see the problem. We would not want an animal to suffer unnecessarily, but does it have a *right* to that (a topic we will discuss in Chapter 7)? A lot of animal suffering (if indeed animals suffer) will be caused by other animals. Lions chase zebras, cats chase birds, birds eat spiders, and so on. The issue is about human behaviour towards animals rather than the rights of the animals. We can say that it is wrong to cause unnecessary pain or distress to animals, but we don't have to invent 'animal rights' to act on this.

What about our consumer behaviour? Does a right to shop cut across the rights of other people? We might largely agree with the UN Universal Declaration of Human Rights but find we are compromising it by our choice of products. For example, if you choose to wear branded sports clothing (*I can't name the companies because they have more expensive lawyers than me*) it is likely that it was made in a developing world sweatshop where people are forced to work long hours without holidays and without reasonable pay. Their basic human rights (according to the UN charter, articles 4, 5, 6, 8, 13, 20, 24, 25) are not being fulfilled. Every time you buy one of these products, however cool they are, you are helping to fuel a modern slave trade.

Box 1.4   An outline of the United Nations Universal Declaration of Human Rights 1948

Article 1. All human beings are born free and equal in dignity and rights.

Article 2. Everyone is entitled to all the rights and freedoms set forth in this Declaration, without distinction of any kind, such as race, colour, sex, language, religion, political or other opinion, national or social origin, property, birth or other status.

Article 3. Everyone has the right to life, liberty and security of person.

Article 4. No one shall be held in slavery or servitude.

Article 5. No one shall be subjected to torture or to cruel, inhuman or degrading treatment.

Article 6. Everyone has the right to recognition everywhere as a person before the law.

Article 7. All are equal before the law.

Article 8. Everyone has the right to an effective remedy by the competent national tribunals for acts violating the fundamental rights granted him by the constitution or by law.

Article 9. No one shall be subjected to arbitrary arrest, detention or exile.

Article 10. Everyone is entitled in full equality to a fair and public hearing by an independent and impartial tribunal.

Article 11. Everyone charged with a penal offence has the right to be presumed innocent until proved guilty.

Article 12. No one shall be subjected to arbitrary interference with his privacy, family, home or correspondence, nor to attacks upon his honour and reputation.

Article 13. Everyone has the right to freedom of movement and residence within the borders of each state.

Article 14. Everyone has the right to seek and to enjoy in other countries asylum from persecution.

Article 15. Everyone has the right to a nationality.

Article 16. Men and women of full age have the right to marry and to found a family. Marriage shall be entered into only with the free and full consent of the intending spouses.

Article 17. Everyone has the right to own property alone as well as in association with others.

Article 18. Everyone has the right to freedom of thought, conscience and religion.

Article 19. Everyone has the right to freedom of opinion and expression.

Article 20. Everyone has the right to freedom of peaceful assembly and association.

Article 21. Everyone has the right to take part in the government of his country. The will of the people shall be the basis of the authority of government; this will be expressed in periodic and genuine elections.

Article 22. Everyone, as a member of society, has the right to social security.

Article 23. Everyone has the right to work.

Article 24. Everyone has the right to rest and leisure, including reasonable limitation of working hours and periodic holidays with pay.

Article 25. Everyone has the right to a standard of living adequate for the health and well-being of himself and of his family, and the right to security in the event of unemployment, sickness, disability, widowhood, old age or other lack of livelihood in circumstances beyond his control. Motherhood and childhood are entitled to special care and assistance.

Article 26. Everyone has the right to free education. Elementary education shall be compulsory.

Article 27. Everyone has the right freely to participate in the cultural life of the community, to enjoy the arts and to share in scientific advancement and its benefits.

Article 28. Everyone is entitled to a social and international order in which the rights and freedoms set forth in this Declaration can be fully realized.

Article 29. Everyone has duties to the community in which alone the free and full development of his personality is possible.

Article 30. Nothing in this Declaration may be interpreted as implying for any State, group or person any right to engage in any activity or to perform any act aimed at the destruction of any of the rights and freedoms set forth herein.

The UK signed up to the European Convention on Human Rights in 1998 and we now have a human rights act as part of the law of the land. If you want to know more about this then you can visit web address (http://news.bbc.co.uk/hi/english/static/in_depth/uk/2000/human_rights/default.stm).

Community or individual rights?

A further issue with the UN Universal Declaration of Human Rights is that it is largely about individual rights rather than community rights. So I might want to freely express hateful ideas, and as an individual it is my right to so, but it cuts across the rights of the community to live in relative harmony and to be free from harassment.

The government of China locks up a large number of political dissidents but it argues that for Chinese society individual rights are less important than collective and social rights. They might well favour the notion that '*the needs of the many outweigh the needs of the few*'.[3] It can be argued that human rights are largely a western idea and we use them to claim the high moral ground while we continue to try and dominate the rest of the world.

Oh, it's a real problem. There are no easy answers here because negotiating and agreeing on how we should behave is a very difficult process. It's difficult enough agreeing who should do the washing up in the house, so agreeing on how we should behave in society is almost impossible. The fact that we largely manage to agree on a code that allows the relatively smooth running of our world is remarkable. The discussion about how we should behave towards each other is one that can never end, and each generation has to re-establish how it believes we should live. This means that the discussions about rights and morals and ethics must always be open. And this is what makes them 'issues' because there are conflicting values and no simple answers.

Moral and ethical development

In the above examples we have considered whether something is right or wrong and we can see this as a moral debate. Morals are something that everyone has and uses to govern their everyday behaviour. We start developing our sense of right and wrong from a very early age and over the course of our lives we structure our behaviour by a moral code. Sometimes we break our own code but by and large people live by rules that make much of their behaviour predictable and socially acceptable. This moral code is rarely written down or put up for discussion.

The term ethics, on the other hand is commonly used to refer to a specific set of rules or guidelines that have been developed by a particular group of people, such as doctors, solicitors or psychologists. These rules are affected by the moral code of the society these people work in. Morals, and therefore ethical codes, are affected by culture and so change from one culture to another and from one period of time to another.

A number of psychologists have written about how we learn right from wrong and how we develop our moral code. Some might see it as a matter of learning which behaviour gets rewarded and which gets punished. This is a **behaviourist** account of morals. Some psychologists make a **psychoanalytic** explanation and look at how the child internalises the personality of their parents.

The most commonly described theories in introductory texts are the **cognitive developmental** accounts that emphasise how we think through problems to arrive at our judgement. The work of Kohlberg (1978), for example, looks at how children develop their ability to reason. He argues that they develop from behaviour based on self-interest to behaviour based on principle. At the earliest level (pre-conventional) they defer to adults and obey rules to gain rewards or avoid punishments. At the next level (conventional) their behaviour is guided by the opinions of other people and by the desire to conform. In the highest level (post-conventional) behaviour is guided by abstract moral principles that go beyond the laws of society. Our choice of moral code will affect our personal response to an ethical code.

Legal requirements and professional standards

Ethical guidelines are not legal requirements. A person cannot be sent to prison if they infringe the ethical code of their professional group. They may be punished by their peers and/or debarred from practising as a professional anymore. One of the distinguishing features of any professional group is its commitment to be self-regulating, as in policing ethical standards. Having said that, it has to be acknowledged that professional groups in this country are very reluctant to act against any of their members. The General Medical Council (GMC) rarely strikes off a doctor, even when gross misconduct has been established, and doctors who behave badly commonly receive only a censure. It can also be argued that psychologists commonly break their own code without being censured, but we'll come on to that later. And as for teachers, they have chosen not to regulate their own profession at all.

Some aspects of ethical/moral behaviour are policed by the law of the land. For example, the death of anyone is subject to legal scrutiny, so even the GMC had to remove Harold Shipman from its register of practitioners after police established he had murdered nearly 300 of his patients. You might argue that if the GMC had monitored his behaviour and responded to his drug abuse and to the complaints made against him, to say nothing of the surprising number of death certificates (Ramsey 2001), then the tragedy might not have happened.

The use of animals is controlled by legislation (e.g. The Animals (Scientific Procedures) Act 1986). The testing of drugs in research is also controlled. More recently legislation for stem cell research[4] has been put in place. Any researcher who breaks these laws may be punished like any other criminal (e.g. fines, probation, custodial sentence), and their work stopped.

Principles, guidelines and issues

Many groups of people go beyond legal requirements to develop ethical principles (the moral values that are applied to their particular interests) and the guidelines or code of practice that is developed from these principles. Some sports people have an ethical code; for example, in golf it is unheard of for professional golfers to try and cheat. This is not the same for all sports and 'gamesmanship'[5] or cheating is seen as fair game in professional football. The English Premier League has constant debate about whether a player has feigned an injury or pretended to have been tripped. It is an interesting moral or ethical point that fans respond to cheating with scorn, but only for teams other than their own. If one of their own players wastes time or tries to put off a penalty taker, that is often seen as a bit of a laugh and fair (I refer you to Old Trafford for examples of these activities).

So the principles inform our guidelines and hence our behaviour, but sometimes these principles create some conflict and lead to ethical issues. It is worth noting that there are very few right and wrong answers to ethical questions because we have to come to our own conclusions based on our own morals and our own interpretation of the ethical guidelines we are trying to follow.

Why study ethics?

It is one of the more difficult areas of psychology to study because there are no clear answers. That might well make it one of the more interesting areas for you, or one of the most frustrating. If there are no clear answers it means that you have the opportunity to develop and express your own opinion. As teachers of psychology we find it interesting to watch the development of ethical opinions in our students. Our own opinions have been changed by these debates. When one of the authors (PB) started teaching psychology some of the studies that were commonly used to illustrate psychological research involved cruel and distressing treatments on animals. I told my students about these without much thought. Over the years I found that students became more and more critical of these studies and after a bit of (belated) thought I decided to drop most of them from my teaching and only to use the remaining ones with very strong health warnings.

The study of ethics allows us to reflect on our own behaviour and so change it for the better. It also allows us to reflect on the behaviour of psychologists to give a better understanding of the subject and, most importantly, to give us some great evaluative points for essays.

In the rest of this book we will look further at ethical issues and ethical guidelines. Ethics are often used in a very narrow way in psychology to assess how we carry out our research, but there are some wider ethical issues to consider alongside the practical guidelines. We will consider the special issue of socially sensitive research – this is research that has controversial social consequences. We will also consider the conduct of psychologists and the ways in which some of them continue to behave in ethically dubious ways. Finally, we will consider the issues around using animals in psychological research.

Summary

In this chapter we have considered morals, rights and ethical issues. *Morals* are things that concern right and wrong in human behaviour. It isn't always easy to work out what is right and wrong which gives rise to moral issues. There are no absolutes in the area of moral behaviour – but people have attempted to establish certain universal *rights*. *Ethics* are the morals of a professional group and ethical guidelines or principles are established as a means of helping to resolve ethical issues which arise. In ethics, as in morals, there are often dilemmas about what is clearly right or clearly wrong.

Further reading

Kimmel, A.J. (1996) *Ethical Issues in Behavioural Research*, Oxford: Blackwell. (Many of the issues raised in this chapter, and the rest of the book, are discussed in the book by Kimmel, a classic textbook on ethical issues.)

Websites

The Tuskegee experiment <www.kn.pacbell.com/wired/BHM/tuskegee_quest.html>

The United Nations

Human Rights Act <http://news.bbc.co.uk/hi/english/static/in_depth/uk/2000/human_rights/default.stm>

Ethical issues in classic psychology studies: studies outlined and questions raised about the ethics <http://onlineethics.org/reseth/psychindex.html>

2

Ethical issues in human research

 Ethical principles and the issues they bring up
Justifying unethical research
Summary

In this chapter we will look at ethical issues, that is, the dilemmas that arise when designing psychological research and the moral principles we use to assess whether our psychological research is good or bad, right or wrong. First we will look at some general ethical principles and the issues that arise from them. We will then look at how breaking ethical guidelines can sometimes be justified. Finally we will look at whether we can resolve any of these issues. You will note that there are very few clear-cut judgements to be made and all these issues have many shades of grey.

Ethical principles and the issues they bring up

I observed a mature and initially poised businessman enter the laboratory smiling and confident. Within 20 minutes he was reduced to a twitching, stuttering wreck . . . he constantly pulled his earlobe, and twisted his hands. At one point he pushed his fist into his forehead and muttered: 'Oh my God, let's stop it'.

Yet he continued to respond to every word of the experimenter
(Milgram 1963: 377)

It may seem beyond belief that this is the description of a participant
in a psychology experiment. Why would anyone permit such suffering
to continue? From the participant's view the issue is one of psychological harm. From society's point of view this harm may be balanced
by the potential for increased knowledge which may save or improve
lives. The issue is one of relative morality. The psychologist conducting
the research may be torn between responsibilities towards both the
individual and towards society.

Equally chilling and less well known are the instructions given by
Zimbardo to the experimental participants who had been given the role
of guard in his famous Stanford Prison Experiment. In this study, a
group of ordinary young men were assigned to play the part of guard
or prisoner in a pretend prison set-up in the basement of the psychology
department. This study is commonly believed to show how the uniform
of a guard is enough to create abusive and dominating behaviour in
the people who wear it. The experiment had to be stopped after six
days because of the level of distress in the prisoners, but before you
accept Zimbardo's interpretation of the reason for the bad behaviour
by the guards, you should read his instructions to them:

> You can create in the prisoners feelings of boredom, a sense of
> fear to some degree, you can create a notion of arbitrariness that
> their life is totally controlled by us, by the system, you, me and
> they'll have no privacy . . . They have no freedom of action, they
> can do nothing, say nothing that we don't permit. We're going
> to take away their individuality in various ways. In general
> what all this leads to is a sense of powerlessness. That is, in
> this situation we'll have all the power and they'll have none.
> (Zimbardo 1989, quoted in Haslam and Reicher 2003: 3)

Zimbardo is clearly inciting the pretend guards to behave in abusive
ways, and a close inspection of the above (see Haslam and Reicher
2003) shows that he is putting himself in the role of the leader of this
abuse. Note that he says 'we're going to take away their individuality'
and 'we'll have all the power', thereby including himself as one of the
guards. We'll come back to these two studies in the next chapter where

we'll argue that the Milgram study was in fact largely ethical while the Zimbardo study was not.

This chapter is about ethical issues. Such issues arise because there are things to debate about how psychologists should conduct their research and, indeed, whether they should conduct it at all. It is probably fair to say that both Zimbardo and Milgram carried out their famous studies in good faith. They had serious scientific objectives and they very seriously considered ethical issues before they started and after they had completed the studies. The fact that we are still discussing the ethics of these studies after more than 40 years shows how difficult it is to resolve these issues and come up with clear principles that can be applied to every situation. The next section deals with some ethical principles and gives some examples of the issues and problems that they pose for psychologists.

The participant's view

Respect, autonomy and deception

We would argue that: *all individuals should be treated with respect and allowed to be in control of their own life (autonomous).*

Psychology experiments that involve deception are in danger of taking away a participant's right to autonomy and denying their right to respect. Consider Milgram's classic study of obedience. The purpose of the study was to see whether participants would be willing to administer harmful shocks to a **confederate** if they were instructed to do so by someone in authority. Participants were told they were taking part in a study about methods of learning. The 'shocks' that were administered were painless though the participant (called the 'teacher') was given a demonstration shock to lead him to believe that they would be real.[1] In other words they were deceived about the purpose and nature of the experiment. If they had been told of its true nature, their subsequent behaviour would have been very different. However, they did know that they were taking part in a psychology study and they chose to take part and to continue with the experiment, so you might argue that the deception is not a major issue.

Harm

We would argue that: *individuals should not suffer immediate or long-term harm, either psychological or physical.*

In the case of medical experiments such as the Tuskegee study (see Chapter 1), the potential harm is physical and a number of the experimental subjects died from their lack of medical treatment. In some psychology experiments the participants may experience physical harm. Milgram (1963) reported that three participants experienced 'full-blown uncontrollable seizures'. But for the most part, the biggest risk in psychological experiments is temporary or permanent psychological harm.

Morris Braverman, a 39-year-old social worker, was one of the participants in Milgram's experiment who continued to give shocks until the maximum was reached. When interviewed a year after the experiment he claimed that he had learned something of personal importance as a result of being in the experiment. His wife said, with reference to his willingness to obey orders, 'You can call yourself an Eichman.'[2] Such comments must affect the way an individual feels about himself even if there has been some attempt at self-justification (Milgram 1974).

There are numerous examples of individuals who have special qualities or who have lived in unusual situations and have been studied by psychologists because of their importance for psychological theories. As a result they have sometimes become the victims of psychology. An example of this is the young woman known as Genie. Genie was brought up in terrible conditions for the first 13 years of her life, during which she was continually restrained by her father, often strapped to a chair, and never spoken to. When she was discovered she was unable to speak. She seemed to be an ideal case to use to answer a number of scientific questions about the development of language. Her subsequent care and exploitation by psychologists is a matter of some dispute (Rymer 1993). For years she lived with the family of one of the psychologists who was studying her and she was well cared for. But when the research money ran out Genie was abandoned back into abusive environments. Genie's mother successfully sued some of the psychologists involved for 'extreme, unreasonable, and outrageously intensive testing, experimentation, and observation'. It is argued that concern for psychological research was placed before compassion for the child.

Psychological therapies have provided many people with relief from troubling and harmful symptoms. They have also on occasions produced considerable harm, both psychologically and physically. Among the most controversial of these treatments are the use of some antipsychotic medications and also the use of guided imagery to recover 'lost' memories. Antipsychotic medication, for example, chlorpromazine, has been used to reduce the level of hallucinations and delusions experienced by people suffering from schizophrenia. The medication is relatively successful in reducing these symptoms (WHO 2001) but it has numerous damaging side effects. Some of these side effects, such as tardive dyskinesia, are permanent so even when the patient stops taking the medication they still have unusual behavioural tics (see Box 2.1).

Box 2.1 Side effects of antipsychotic medication

Antipsychotic medication can produce a wide range of side effects ranging from mildly unpleasant to severe and potentially debilitating. Some of the common ones include:

- *Parkinson-like symptoms*. Characterised by muscle rigidity and tremor, people with symptoms of drug-induced Parkinsonism may appear to have fixed facial expressions and speak in slow manner with a monotonous tone. Parkinsonism affects up to four out of ten people on typical neuroleptic medication and older people are more susceptible to the symptoms at lower doses of medication. Symptoms appear within days of starting medication but usually improve spontaneously within three months of treatment.
- *Dystonia*. Sustained muscle contraction, contorting and twisting movements are all signs of dystonia. Spasms are often painful and distressing and can be frightening. In extreme cases, dystonic movements can cause injuries such as dislocated jaw.
- *Akathisia*. Characterised by jittery and restless movements, akathisia literally means 'can't sit down'. It is one of the more common side effects (it affects about a quarter of people on neuroleptic treatment) and can be extremely distressing.
- *Tardive dyskinesia*. Abnormal facial movements, smacking lips, chewing, sucking, twisting the tongue, can all be signs of tardive dyskinesia (TD). Jerky often purposeless limb movements are also characteristic signs.

Approximately one person in five on antipsychotic medication will experience TD, although the incidence increases with prolonged exposure to neuroleptic medication. It often persists after the treatment has stopped and cannot be treated.

- *Neuroleptic malignant syndrome*. Neuroleptic malignant syndrome (NMS) is a very rare yet potentially fatal side effect of neuroleptic medication. Symptoms include movement disorders and an extremely high temperature. It is important to detect the symptoms early in order to treat this condition.
- *Sedation*. This is a common side effect of neuroleptic treatment. Patients may feel tired, lethargic or weak when they are taking antipsychotics such as chlorpromazine.
- *Anticholinergic effects*. A dry mouth, feelings of dizziness or light-headedness, constipation and blurred vision while taking antipsychotics are due to the action of these drugs on cholinergic receptors in the brain and in the rest of the body.
- *Weight gain*. This is a relatively common side effect of antipsychotics and often causes a great deal of distress. It is also associated with health risks such as high blood pressure, diabetes and respiratory problems.

Source: http://www.emental-health.com/

The term 'harm' tends to suggest physical harm, but psychologists can sometimes create serious psychological harm even when they have the best of intentions. Look at the false memory/recovered memory debate. If you want to check out a major controversy in psychology then look up 'false memory syndrome' on the internet. In the UK, cognitive psychologist Elizabeth Loftus is mainly famous for her experimental work on eyewitness testimony. In the USA she is the subject of a very hostile debate because of her work on false memories. She challenged the use of guided imagery therapy (amongst others) to 'discover' memories of child abuse that were previously unknown to the patient. As a result of her scientific work as well as her activity within the legal system, public and professional opinion is gradually coming to realise that such memories, however compelling they may seem when related by a witness, are sometimes the product of recent reconstructive memory processes rather than of past objective reality. That is, the events did not happen and a 'memory' has been created during the sessions with the therapist. Numerous law suits have now been won against therapists who encouraged clients to believe in fictitious episodes of child abuse (Lynn *et al.* 2003).

The dilemma that comes out of this work is painful and almost impossible to resolve. It is clear that some children suffer physical and sexual abuse and that some of them do not report this until they are adults, if they ever do. When they report it, some of their memories might be sketchy and their recall might improve with help from a therapist. But what about the adult who has no memories of childhood abuse who now 'remembers' in therapy some abusive behaviours? Where did these memories come from? Are they recovered or false? Get this wrong and there is great potential for harm. The major problem with this debate is that people often have very fixed positions, which is why Elizabeth Loftus has become a hate figure to those who will not accept any other explanation than their own (Loftus 1998).

Privacy

We would argue that: *what you do and say should not be exposed to public scrutiny without your permission.*

Westin (1968) defines privacy as 'the claim of individuals, groups, or institutions to determine for themselves when, how and to what extent information about them is communicated to others'. An illustration of this issue can be seen in the 'tearoom trade' study by Laud Humphreys (1970). Humphreys sought to demonstrate that certain common prejudices about homosexuals were mistaken. To do these he pretended to be a 'watchqueen' in a 'tearoom'. A 'tearoom' is a public toilet where men meet for sex with other men. A 'watchqueen' is someone who is allowed to watch the sexual activity and in exchange acts as a lookout. When apparently watching out for danger Humphreys also made a note of the licence plate numbers of the visitors to the tearoom. He was later able to access the addresses of the car owners and interviewed them at home, claiming to be a health services worker. After this he destroyed the record of any individuals' names. The main finding of this study was that most of the men involved in the tearoom trade led the rest of their lives as heterosexuals, often living with their wives. This confirms the common finding (for example, Kinsey *et al.* 1948) that the proportion of people who *only* have same-sex relationships is relatively small, but the

27

proportion of people who *sometimes* have same-sex relationships is much larger. Humphreys might argue that he had protected the privacy of his participants by destroying the names, but you can also argue that he had invaded their right to privacy by observing them and by obtaining further information from them through the use of deception.

Privacy is a big issue at the start of the twenty-first century. In some ways we do not expect to have a great deal of privacy and, on the whole, we do not appear to be too bothered about it. Your mobile phone is a tracking device so you can be located whenever it is on. The company keeps a record of your calls, both incoming and outgoing. A recent development of software to track phone calls (WatCall produced by Harlequin Ltd) can analyse telephone records and is able to compare numbers that are dialled and received in order to group users into 'friendship networks'. The software avoids the normal legal requirements needed for phone tapping (Euronet 1998).

In public space you also do not have much privacy. Britain has the largest closed circuit television (cctv) network in the world. There are at least 2.5 million cameras across the country and, in the course of a typical day, the average city dweller can expect to be filmed at least eight times. If they are very unlucky, or lucky depending on your point of view, they may be filmed 300 times. In London alone there are 150,000 cameras, used by the police as well as businesses and other private organisations, keeping a watchful eye over the capital (*The Guardian*, 1 August 2001). This cctv footage records your behaviour when you do not expect it and can sometimes be shown for entertainment or profit. There are some attempts to restrict this: for example, a man whose suicide attempt was captured by his local council's cctv cameras and released to newspapers and television companies won his legal action at the European Court of Human Rights in 2003. The court ruled that Mr X's right to respect for his private life had been violated by the broadcast of the cctv footage. Mr X said his life had been shattered since a film taken of him in Brentwood High Street, Essex in August 1995, with a kitchen knife, about to slash his wrists, was shown to more than nine million viewers in 1996 on BBC TV's *Crime Beat*. He was severely depressed after losing his job and learning that his partner, the mother of his daughter, had been diagnosed as terminally ill (*The Guardian*, 29 January 2003).

It is clear that privacy has to be respected by psychologists, but it is neither clear how much privacy people expect nor how much they will be allowed by the press, surveillance techniques and also by each other. Oh, and just in case you think that what you do at home is private, then you might like to know that the Google search engine is able to keep a record of what you search on the internet (see www.google-watch.org). The company has links to the current US administration (George W. Bush) and US Defense Department. They know where you live and they know what you are doing there.

Subjects and participants

We would argue that: *research should be a collaborative process between researcher and participant not an autocratic one of ruler and subject, the term used in the past to refer to a research participant.*

A further issue for participants is the balance of power in the research setting. Typically the researcher holds the power in the research setting because he or she knows what the experiment is about and the procedures to be followed. This often leaves the 'subject' powerless. This power relationship is reflected in the use of the term 'subject' for the research participants other than the researcher. The concept of a 'subject' may encourage researchers to be less sensitive to the needs and rights of individuals involved in research. During the 1990s there was a move to use the term 'participant' instead of 'subject' in order to reflect the active involvement of participants and to emphasise their important rights.

It is to be hoped that the change of the term from 'subject' to 'participant' is more than just cosmetic. It is not a good idea to rewrite the old studies and start calling the subjects 'participants', because they weren't. They were treated as passive respondents to the experimental situations set up by psychologists and they were rarely dealt with as collaborators.

This issue cuts very deep into the power relationship between the expert (in this case psychologist) and the naive (in this case the general public). If we say that psychological research should improve human life (see below), then we should include ordinary people in the process and inform them of what we are doing. Mind you, there's not a lot of money to be made out of that. It is much more profitable to invent something that people were doing fine without but have now come to believe is essential and then sell it to them. Our world is full of useless products that are testament to this process. Consider the role of the bereavement counsellor. Up until the last 20 years or so there was no such thing as a bereavement counsellor, though human beings have been dealing with death for two million years relatively successfully. They have found ways to make sense of it and to comfort each other. Suddenly, this does not seem to be adequate and we need a qualification to discuss bereavement issues. You might argue that psychologists are attempting to hijack everyday skills and then sell them back to us. Part of the collaboration ethic requires us not to exploit people for profit.

On the other hand, you could argue that these 'psychological products' are necessary as a consequence of changed communities and lifestyles. In the past, close-knit families and communities offered mutual support. Today professionals take on such roles in the more urban and isolated communities we live in.

The profession's view

We would argue that: *members of any professional group have a duty to protect the integrity of that group.*

Imagine a make-believe country where it is known that most doctors are not to be trusted and often don't care whether their diagnosis is right or wrong (*Are you sure this is make believe? – ed*). There are a few doctors who cling to their ethical principles and are very concerned to conduct themselves properly and with regard for their patients. However, they realise that few patients will believe them unless they get rid of the bad doctors themselves. People need to trust the *profession* as well as the *individual* doctor, so in this country we have the General Medical Council (GMC) to ensure that all doctors behave correctly and adequately. To be fair, the GMC did eventually strike Harold Shipman off the register after he was convicted of murdering hundreds of his patients, so nothing to worry about there.

Psychologists need to be concerned about the ethical treatment of participants in order to ensure that psychology continues to be seen in a good light, and so that individuals will continue to be willing to participate in psychology experiments. We'll come back to this issue in Chapter 4. Psychologists (and other researchers) also need to be concerned about fraudulent behaviour, which could bring the profession into disrepute. One of the best known examples of this is the work of Sir Cyril Burt. Burt and his researchers reported data on the IQ of twins and used this to argue that individual differences in intelligence were largely inherited. Burt was a highly respected and influential psychologist and no one suspected that he might have invented his data until Kamin (1974), among others, pointed out a variety of inaccuracies and inconsistencies. It was also discovered that two of Burt's supposed collaborators apparently had never existed. By this time Burt was dead and therefore not able to defend himself. Others have subsequently suggested that the accusations were exaggerated and some errors were simply due to carelessness (Joynson 1989). See website details at the end of the chapter if you wish to read more about this. The remarkable things about this case are the very obvious flaws in these data and the many years that the data went unchallenged. It reflects badly on the process of scientific review that is meant to ensure that only the best work is published.

Lack of honesty in reporting research may be more of a pervasive problem than many psychologists would care to admit. In journal articles methods sections are commonly incomplete (Banyard and Hunt 2000) and omit details about who the research is conducted on, how they were selected and where the research was carried out. Result sections commonly report on the significance of results without stating the size of the effect (Clarke-Carter 1997). For example, imagine a smoking reduction programme that shows a statistically significant effect. This might encourage people to take part in the programme, but what if the average number of cigarettes smoked per week had only dropped from 160 to 155? The programme has had a measurable effect but no real effect on the health or behaviour of the participants.

It would appear that lack of detail in reporting research and distortions in the conclusions go relatively unreported. If a psychologist decided to comment on the behaviour and research of a colleague they might well be seen as a 'whistle-blower'. The issue of whistle-blowing (on your colleagues) goes against one of the strongest playground ethics: *don't snitch*. As a result, it is rare for doctors to be called to book (see page 17) and the major frauds or malpractice cases are more likely to be exposed by people outside the field of study rather than by their peers.

Society's view

We would argue that: *the purpose of conducting any research is to establish knowledge that may be used to improve the world in which we live or to better understand ourselves and our behaviour.*

Research rarely sets out its aims as being to make the world a better place but, ultimately, that is the goal (*you wish! – ed*). From society's viewpoint the ethical issue is a utilitarian one – balance costs against benefits. 'Society' places greater emphasis on the benefits in contrast with individuals who pay greater attention to the costs. Even this apparently clear and worthy ambition has a difficult side to it. We might believe that the world would be a better place if there was, for example, more order, less crime, less waste and less anger. We might be able to achieve these through behavioural, medical or even surgical interventions, but in so doing we might well cut across individual rights in the pursuit of the greater good for the community. And that's what creates an ethical *issue* – trying to decide whose rights are uppermost or more compromised.

An illustration of this dilemma can be seen in the school choice made by parents. In Nottingham (where one of the authors lives) it is estimated that around 50 per cent of all secondary school aged pupils go to schools outside their catchment area (personal communication). This represents a general exodus from city schools by children with professional parents. If all these children were schooled in their catchment areas then the pressure from these vocal parents might well improve the schools and help the community in which they live. This would be the socially responsible choice. If, however, you take the individual rather than the social view then you look to the personal advancement of your children regardless of the consequences for the people who live around you and you send them out of catchment to a 'better' school.

So far we have looked at the ethical principles from the viewpoint of the participant, the professional and the general public. We will now go on to look at the issues that arise with a range of research techniques or locations.

Justifying unethical research

Deception, invasion of privacy and harm to participants are all considered to be unethical, but are there situations in which such a lack of ethical behaviour is acceptable? There are many ways of dealing with ethical issues – such as the use of guidelines, a strategy that is examined in the next chapter. Psychologists also deal with ethical issues by justifying their work.

Some forms of deception aren't that bad

In many studies the deception that is practised is actually very minor. For example, in many memory studies the participants are not informed beforehand that they will be required to recall information. This is to prevent the participants from rehearsing the information.

In some field experiments the task undertaken by participants is relatively harmless. For example, Bickman (1974) investigated obedience by arranging for male experimenters to dress as either a milkman, a guard, or in a sports jacket and tie. The experimenter then gave orders to 153 randomly selected pedestrians in Brooklyn, New York. The participants were asked either to pick up some litter, give the experimenter a dime for a parking meter, or stand on the other side of a bus stop. The study found that people were more likely to obey instructions from someone in a uniform and most likely to obey the guard. The deception is that the members of the public believe they are dealing with an embarrassing social confrontation from an unknown and unpredictable person. They might reasonably follow the instruction as it is the least line of resistance and the most adaptive thing to do. Is such an intervention harmless?

Christiansen (1988) reports that participants don't seem to object to deception as long as it is not extreme. You might, however, still challenge the Bickman study because it is hard to see what scientific purpose it serves nor how it contributes to the common good. If you were a participant in this experiment how would you imagine you would feel? This means of assessing ethical issues in a study is called using **presumptive consent**. In other words, you cannot ask the actual participants to give their informed consent because this would spoil the experiment, but you can ask a similar group of people and then *presume* that the actual participants would feel the same way.

Validity of research data

The reason that deception is sometimes used in laboratory experiments is that the research would simply not make sense if participants were not deceived, as in Milgram's obedience study. When conducting field experiments, deception is sometimes unavoidable. Is the answer that one should not conduct field experiments? The main reason to conduct field experiments instead of laboratory experiments is to investigate more true-to-life behaviour. In a laboratory people do not behave in the same way as they do in the 'real world' for a variety of reasons – because a laboratory is an artificial environment and participants' behaviour is governed by an unrealistic set of rules, or because participants know they are in a research study and respond to cues about how to behave (**demand characteristics**). We say that these studies lack **mundane realism** and may lack **ecological validity**. This means that field experiments commonly have greater validity and the price we pay is deception.

Costs and benefits

The main method of justifying unethical practices is with reference to the consequences of the research – a utilitarian approach to ethics. If we can see that a study has the potential to produce meaningful findings that can be used to enhance human lives, then we can balance this against possible costs. It can be argued that the Milgram study has given us an invaluable insight into the nature of evil and tyranny, and it is an insight that continues to shock even 50 years after the original study. We would argue that it is one of psychology's most important studies for that very reason. It is difficult to use the 'invaluable insight' defence very often in psychology because studies that are as challenging and informative as the Milgram study are as rare as a sunny day in Manchester.

Can we predict costs and benefits?

It is difficult if not impossible to predict both costs and benefits prior to conducting a study. Milgram asked a group of 110 students, psychiatrists and other adults to predict how participants would behave in his obedience study. The majority said that 150 volts would be the limit – a strong shock. The maximum predicted was 300 volts, just below 'extreme intensity shock'. In actual fact the majority (65 per cent) of the participants gave the maximum shock of 450 volts. This shows how inaccurate prior estimates can be. In fact Milgram called his (1963) article 'A *Behavioural* Study of Obedience' (our italics). He wasn't interested in what people *thought* they would do, but in what they actually *did*.

Can we measure costs and benefits?

It is difficult to quantify costs and benefits even after the study. How does one quantify costs and benefits? How much does personal distress cost? If the results of a study demonstrate that people are more likely to obey someone in uniform, how much is that benefit? How do we cope with the fact that each participant experiences a different cost in the same experiment? For example, in Milgram's study some of the participants appeared to be relatively untroubled by the experience and some reported afterwards that they were glad to have participated because it taught them something important. Does this make the deception less 'costly'?

Who does the counting?

Costs and benefits add up differently depending on who is doing the counting. If we judge the costs and benefits from a participant's point of view, we might list distress and loss of time versus financial rewards and a feeling of having contributed to scientific research. The research has other costs and benefits, such as possible loss of self-respect for participants versus professional success. Finally, society might weigh up the potential distress of people in certain situations against the use of any knowledge to better human lives.

Who wins?

Cost-benefit analysis tends to ignore the rights of individuals in favour of practical considerations. The judgement about costs and benefits is made by the researcher or other professionals who sit on an ethical committee (see page 36). A researcher may well overestimate the benefits of his/her work and underestimate any potential harm to participants. This is exactly why researchers are encouraged by the BPS guidelines to seek the views of their colleagues.

Is the cost benefit analysis useful?

Cynics might argue that the cost-benefit calculation raises as many ethical issues as it is meant to resolve. Diana Baumrind (1975, see Study Aids summary pages 142–4) argued that the cost-benefit approach was developed as a means of dealing with moral dilemmas but, in fact, one is left with another set of dilemmas. Thus the approach doesn't actually resolve the problem. Baumrind also argued that the cost-benefit approach in a way legitimises unethical practices. For example it suggests that deception and harm *are* acceptable in many situations – if the benefits are great enough.

> **Progress exercise**
>
> Select two or more psychological studies that you have learned about in your psychology course (such as Zimbardo's prison study) and present arguments to explain in what way the procedures are unethical and in what way you could justify the use of such procedures.

Resolving ethical issues

Justifying unethical research is one way to deal with ethical issues. There are other ways to try to resolve the problems created by ethical issues, which are briefly described below.

Ethical committees

Ethical committees are used in order to avoid bias when a researcher is left to make his or her own ethical judgements about a prospective research study. Most institutions (e.g. universities, research units) in which research is carried out now have their own ethical committee, which considers all research proposals from the perspective of the rights and dignity of the participants. The existence of such committees helps to correct the power imbalance between experimenter and participant. However, if all the members of an ethical committee are researchers in psychology, they may be disinclined to turn down proposals from professional colleagues. For this and other reasons, it is desirable for every ethical committee to include some non-psychologists and at least one non-expert member of the public.

A good example of how an ethics panel can deal with difficult issues is illustrated by work on *The Experiment* (Haslam and Reicher 2003, see Study Aids summary pages 142–4). This televised prison simulation experiment (described page 60 this text) wrestled with all the complex issues of harm, informed consent, etc. The report of the ethics panel can be found on the website (http://www.stetay.com/experiment/fullreport.html).

However, ethical committees are only effective if they meet. In some cases a researcher can talk the research proposal round to each member of the committee and stand over them as they make their decision. This puts the balance of power with the researcher not the committee.

1. Work with one or two other students and devise a study to investigate obedience to authority (or you could select a different behaviour). Record the details of the design you would use.
2. Appoint some members of your class to act as an ethical committee and ask them to consider whether or not your proposed study is ethically acceptable. The committee might (a) decide whether or not the study should be given permission to go ahead; (b) outline any conditions that would have to be met before the study could go ahead.

Progress exercise

Use of ethical guidelines

Professional groups develop ethical codes of conduct that are a set of rules which can and should be followed by members of the professional group. These codes of conduct or guidelines are discussed in detail in the next chapter. There are two particular items found in ethical guidelines that may help to resolve ethical objections: debriefing and the right to withdraw.

Debriefing

It is commonplace for participants to be **debriefed** after an experiment. This gives the researcher an opportunity to assess the effects of the research procedures and offer some form of counselling if necessary. The researcher may also use this as an opportunity to find out more from the participant in relation to the research. For example, Milgram asked participants if they suspected the real purpose of the study.

Once the participant has been correctly informed about the aim of the experiment they may elect to withhold their data from the study. In a sense they are exercising their right to informed consent in retrospect.

Right to withdraw

All participants should be advised at the start of a research study that they can withdraw from the study at any time. This means that if the participant does feel harmed or undermined in any way, he or she can quit. In practice this is not that simple. A participant may be being paid for participation and may feel that quitting isn't a real option. Even if participants are not paid they may feel awkward about asking to be excused. Many psychological studies use students as participants. Such students may not feel that they can jeopardise their course standing by harming the ongoing study.

Ways to gain consent without asking

Some researchers seek presumptive general consent, as outlined earlier. Another method is **prior general consent**, as used by Gamson *et al.* (1982), where participants were given a list of research projects including one that involved deception. They generally consent to the research study, not realising entirely what the implications were (see pages 69–70 for a description).

Alternatives: role play

It is possible to fully inform the participants about the nature of the study and then ask them to *pretend* that they are actually participating in an experiment. This is what Zimbardo did in his prison study (see page 59) and there is good evidence that both prisoners and guards took their roles very seriously, apparently forgetting that it was only make believe. The prisoners took to referring to each other by number even when they knew they weren't being observed. The guards became overzealous in their roles, some even volunteering to do extra hours without pay.

On the other hand, it has also been argued that even though the prisoners and guards took their roles seriously they were actually only behaving according to stereotypes about prisoner/guard behaviour that they had learned from films; that is, they were behaving according to social norms. If this was real life rather than role play, people would be more likely to derive their behaviour from personal rather than social norms. This means that we have to be careful about the conclusions we draw from the research.

In general Kimmel (1996) concludes that role playing has not offered a viable alternative to experimental research though there have been some successes. For example, Greenberg (1967) repeated a study first conducted by Schachter (1959). In the original study some participants were told that they were going to receive painful electric shocks, while others had no reason to believe the experiment would be stressful. Schachter found that those expecting shocks were more likely to seek the company of others who they thought were also anxious, supporting the hypothesis that 'misery loves (miserable) company'. In the replication, participants were told the details of the experiment and asked to act as if it was real. The findings were similar though not significant. However, Kimmel reports that such successes have been limited.

Summary

Ethical issues are discussed and developed so that we can come to some agreement about principles for good behaviour. These principles affect our everyday life but in this text we are most concerned with how they affect the conduct of psychology. From the comfort of our armchairs it is possible to rip up a lot of psychology as unethical (and it is jolly good fun to do so). When psychologists get their hands dirty by actually carrying out studies and attempting to discover things about our behaviour and experience, then they have to deal with a range of complex ethical dilemmas. There are very few simple answers and many ideas about how to deal with the dilemmas – such as justifying unethical practices, use of ethical committees and role play. Possibly the most important way is the use of ethical principles and guidelines, which are examined in the next chapter.

Further reading

Baumrind, D. (1964) Some thoughts on ethics of research: after reading Milgram's behavioural study of obedience, *American Psychologist* 19, 421–3. (Read the original article to get a feel for ethical issues. Give this reference to your local library who will obtain a photocopy for a small fee.)

Websites

Adolf Eichman <www.pbs.org/eichmann/>

Cyril Burt <www.indiana.edu/~intell/burtaffair.shtml>

Websites related to the research by Milgram and Zimbardo are described on page 63.

3

Ethical principles and guidelines

What are ethical principles and guidelines?
Limitations of ethical principles as a way of resolving
   ethical issues
Summary

This chapter is about how psychologists deal with ethical issues by trying to develop principles and guidelines for psychologists to follow. A lot of time is put into ethics and, on the surface at least, psychologists take ethics very seriously. The problem comes with the interpretation of the principles and clash of interests that can occur. In this chapter we will look at these problems and try to unpick some of the complexities in the discussion. The first thing we must do is to see how these principles match up to the issues we identified in Chapter 2. We will then go on to consider what other principles could or should have been included, and what happens when psychologists fail to adhere to these principles.

What are ethical principles and guidelines?

Ethical principles are intended to be a guide for individuals on how to behave in situations that raise ethical issues. One of the minor problems to clear up is the use of terms like guidelines and principles. We have already written about this in Chapter 1 (see Box 1.2) and tried to suggest a distinction between all the terms. Unfortunately, as we pointed out, the different organisations use the terms in different ways. Try not to get too confused or worried about the distinctions between 'principles' and 'guidelines': the important thing is the argument rather than the definitions.

The BPS ethical principles

The British Psychological Society (BPS), like many psychological societies, has published a set of principles and guidelines (see Box 3.1 for a summary). These principles and guidelines spell out a code of behaviour for all psychologists working in the UK. This includes practising psychologists (for example, those involved in treating patients with mental disorders or psychologists working in industry advising on how to improve performance) as well as research psychologists.

The BPS Code of Conduct (BPS 2000) contains a variety of different documents relating to different activities that psychologists engage in and responsibilities that they have; for example, work with animals, guidelines about advertising the services offered by psychologists, and an equal opportunities policy statement. There are papers on sexual harassment at work and the difficult issue of dual relationships. Dual relationships are defined as occurring when a psychologist has two types of relationships with the same person, one as a psychologist and one or more other relationships such as uncle or employer or boyfriend. At the end of the document there are also guidelines for good practice in the use of penile plethysmography, but we don't want to go there (*certainly not – ed*). If you're interested you can look at the BPS website (www.bps.org.uk/). The code of conduct includes a set of 11 principles for conducting research with human participants. We will have a brief look at the principles in turn.

1. *Introduction*

    Good psychological research is only possible if there is mutual respect and confidence between investigators and participants. Ethical

**Box 3.1   Summary of the British Psychological Society
'Ethical principles for conducting research with human
participants' (BPS 2000)**

1. **Introduction**. Good psychological research is only possible if there is mutual respect and confidence between investigators and participants. Ethical guidelines are necessary to clarify the conditions under which psychological research is acceptable.

2. **General**. The essential principle is that the investigation should be considered from the standpoint of all participants; foreseeable threats to their psychological well-being, health, values or dignity should be eliminated. It should be borne in mind that the best judge of whether an investigation will cause offence may be members of the population from which the participants in the research are to be drawn.

3. **Consent**. The investigator should inform the participants of all aspects of the research or intervention that might reasonably be expected to influence willingness to participate.

4. **Deception**. The withholding of information or the misleading of participants is unacceptable if the participants are typically likely to object or show unease once debriefed.

5. **Debriefing**. In studies where the participants are aware that they have taken part in an investigation, when the data have been collected, the investigator should provide the participants with any necessary information to complete their understanding of the nature of the research. The investigator should discuss with the participants their experience of the research in order to monitor any unforeseen negative effects or misconceptions.

6. **Withdrawal from the investigation**. At the onset of the investigation investigators should make plain to participants their right to withdraw from the research at any time, irrespective of whether or not payment or other inducement has been offered.

7. **Confidentiality**. Subject to the requirements of legislation, information obtained about a participant during an investigation is confidential unless otherwise agreed in advance. Investigators who are put under pressure to disclose confidential information should draw this point to the attention of those exerting such pressure.

8. **Protection of participants**. Investigators have a primary responsibility to protect participants from physical and mental harm during the

investigation. Normally the risk of harm must be no greater than in ordinary life, i.e. participants should not be exposed to risks greater than or additional to those encountered in their normal lifestyles.

9. **Observational research**. Studies based upon observation must respect the privacy and psychological well-being of the individuals studied. Unless those being observed give their consent to being observed, observational research is only acceptable in situations where those observed would expect to be observed by strangers.

10. **Giving advice**. During research, an investigator may obtain evidence of psychological or physical problems of which a participant is apparently unaware. In such a case the investigator has a responsibility to inform the participant if the investigator believes that by not doing so the participant's future well-being may be endangered.

11. **Colleagues**. A psychologist who believes that another psychologist or investigator may be conducting research that is not in accordance with the principles above should encourage that investigator to re-evaluate the research.

guidelines are necessary to clarify the conditions under which psychological research is acceptable.

The opening paragraphs set the scene for the principles and guidelines and note that although psychologists might be interested in all aspects of human behaviour and experience, there may be some that are off limits because of ethical considerations. It refers the reader to the general **code of conduct** for psychologists and warns about the possibility of legal action by participants whose rights are infringed in research.

2. *General*

The essential principle is that the investigation should be considered from the standpoint of all participants; foreseeable threats to their psychological well-being, health, values or dignity should be eliminated. It should be borne in mind that the best judge of whether an investigation will cause offence may be members of the population from which the participants in the research are to be drawn.

This item points psychologists towards the general public for judgement on their studies. It specifically raises the issue that in our ethnically diverse society the researchers may not have enough knowledge about the participants to understand the implications of psychological research.

3. Consent

The investigator should inform the participants of all aspects of the research or intervention that might reasonably be expected to influence willingness to participate.

This principle says that particular attention should be given to gaining real consent from:

- children and their parents (or from those in loco parentis – that is, people who are acting on behalf of parents such as teachers)
- adults with impairments where they may not fully understand the nature of the study
- people who are detained, for example, in prisons or psychiatric hospitals.

It also asks psychologists to be aware that they are often in a position of authority over their participants. This is the case in the many studies that are conducted by lecturers on students. The use of payments must not be used to encourage someone to take part in harmful or distressing research. You can see how dangerous this can be on the reality television shows that offer cash prizes for people to do dangerous or humiliating things. Finally, this principle also suggests that longitudinal research may require real consent to be given on more than one occasion.

4. Deception

The withholding of information or the misleading of participants is unacceptable if the participants are typically likely to object or show unease once debriefed.

The principle suggests that participants should never be deliberately misled without extremely strong scientific or medical justification. The most important criteria is that information which might affect a participant's decision to continue should not be withheld whereas withholding non-consequential information is not important. Of course, in the field of medicine, deception is a necessary part of treatment trials (for example, when testing the efficacy of a new drug) because the use of **placebos** requires deception. The principle requires researchers to consider possible alternatives before going ahead with a study that involves deception.

5. *Debriefing*

In studies where the participants are aware that they have taken part in an investigation, when the data has been collected, the investigator should provide the participants with any necessary information to complete their understanding of the nature of the research. The investigator should discuss with the participants their experience of the research in order to monitor any unforeseen negative effects or misconceptions.

This principle notes that the use of debriefing does not provide a justification for breaking other ethical principles.

6. *Withdrawal from the investigation*

At the onset of the investigation investigators should make plain to participants their right to withdraw from the research at any time, irrespective of whether or not payment or other inducement has been offered.

This principle extends beyond the completion of the study so the participant should have the right to withdraw their data from the study at any time, including the destruction of any recordings.

7. *Confidentiality*

Subject to the requirements of legislation, information obtained about a participant during an investigation is confidential unless otherwise agreed in advance. Investigators who are put under pressure to disclose confidential information should draw this point to the attention of those exerting such pressure.

The participants of research have a reasonable expectation that they will not be identifiable in the report of the study.

8. Protection of participants

Investigators have a primary responsibility to protect participants from physical and mental harm during the investigation. Normally the risk of harm must be no greater than in ordinary life, i.e. participants should not be exposed to risks greater than or additional to those encountered in their normal lifestyles.

Harm can arise in a number of ways and not all of them can be anticipated. Researchers are asked to be aware of participants' personal circumstances because in some cases this might increase the risks for them in the research. The risks might be physical such as a heart condition or emotional such as a recent bereavement. Also, researchers are asked to exercise caution when discussing the results of studies, especially with parents, because people sometimes put a lot of weight on the words of psychologists. For example, if you took part in a test on personality and the test gave you a high score on the '*Useless Loser Scale*' (made up name, we hope), you might be a bit distressed and take some negative feelings away from the study even though you know that psychometric measures are not always reliable or valid.

9. Observational research

Studies based upon observation must respect the privacy and psychological well-being of the individuals studied. Unless those being observed give their consent to being observed, observational research is only acceptable in situations where those observed would expect to be observed by strangers.

Additional consideration should also be given to local cultural values and the possibility of intruding on the privacy of people who may believe they are unobserved. The words 'confidentiality' and 'privacy' are sometimes used interchangeably, but there is a distinction between the two. Confidentiality concerns the communication of personal information from one person to another, and the trust that this information will then be protected. Privacy refers to a zone of inaccessibility of mind or body, and the trust that this will not be 'invaded'. In other words, we have a right of privacy. If this is invaded confidentiality should be respected.

10. *Giving advice*

(a) *During research, an investigator may obtain evidence of psychological or physical problems of which a participant is apparently unaware. In such a case the investigator has a responsibility to inform the participant if the investigator believes that by not doing so the participant's future well-being may be endangered.*

(b) *If, in the normal course of psychological research a participant asks for advice concerning educational, personality, behavioural or health issues, caution should be exercised. If the issue is serious and the investigator is not qualified to offer assistance, the appropriate source of professional advice should be recommended.*

Advice is a tricky area for psychologists. In very unusual circumstances they might come across some information during a research project that suggests the participant would benefit from professional help. In these circumstances the researcher should tell the participant and suggest some possible sources of help. It is not appropriate, however, for the researcher to start giving advice outside their area of expertise. Say, for example, during an interview a participant becomes emotional and brings up distressing material, it is unlikely that the researcher is a trained counsellor and able to deal effectively with this.

The problem is that if a friend of yours is upset and wants to talk to you then it doesn't matter that you are not a counsellor. You talk to them as a friend. However, if you have been introduced to someone as a psychologist, then they might well have unrealistic expectations about your knowledge and skill to deal with emotional problems.

11. *Colleagues*

A psychologist who believes that another psychologist or investigator may be conducting research that is not in accordance with the principles above should encourage that investigator to re-evaluate the research.

Ethical responsibility is shared and cannot just be placed on the shoulders of one researcher.

Comments on the BPS ethical principles

In the above section we have given a summary of the BPS principles and guidelines. We will now go on to comment on them. This means, inevitably, that we will be interpreting the principles from our own perspective and showing our own concerns and biases. You might well have a different view.

Truly informed consent

The principle that causes most difficulty surrounds the issue of consent. What do we mean by real consent and can we ever be fully informed about anything? The point about research, as Milgram noted, is that we don't know what is going to happen. If we did, there would be no point in the research. Therefore we cannot fully inform our participants. If we carry out simple studies devoid of any relevance to everyday life then it might be possible to identify all the necessary information to achieve real consent, but if we want to investigate how people conduct themselves in real situations we can never achieve this. If the consequence of this is that psychologists are doomed to carry out detailed studies of not very much then their work will become 'impeccable trivia' (Haslam and Reicher 2003). Maybe we have to face the issue of consent head-on and recognise that we can never have fully informed consent. We will look at some examples of studies that have confronted this issue later in this chapter.

There is also the question of whether people actually listen to the information given to them prior to a study. When you have to sign a form that ends 'I agree to abide by the rules above' do you actually read the rules? This is a particular problem with research conducted on the internet. It is the same problem we have with instructions for new equipment: we never read them until we have broken it.

Even if the information is conveyed to a prospective participant they may not fully understand the implications. Knowing that you are about to answer questions which may be of a personal nature does not mean one understands *how* personal these are or what the effects will be.

Deception

> *Psychologists always lie!* (Anonymous student quoted by Kimmel 1996)

With regard to deception, it has to be said that most human interaction is based on a certain amount of deceit. We rarely disclose the truth, the whole truth and nothing but the truth. Imagine what you tell your parents and then your friends about your holiday in Kavos. Both stories are mainly true, but they are likely to be very different. You're not lying, just being selective. In everyday life we don't expect to be told the whole truth, nor do we commonly want it. When we ask someone 'How are you?', we certainly do not want to be told their current medical and psychiatric condition. 'Fine thanks' is the answer we require. We expect to be told the necessary information, not the full works. This book is a case in point. We have not reproduced the full version of the ethical principles of the BPS but have selected what we think are the parts you will find most useful in your studies. Are we deceiving you? Probably not, but we are not giving you full disclosure.

There is also the question of active versus passive deception. In some studies, participants are actively deceived – that is they are told a deliberate lie to lead them away from guessing its true purpose (as in Milgram's experiment). In other studies passive deception takes place when a participant does not know they are being observed, or where researchers provide an incomplete explanation of their research project to participants because of the potential effects. For example, in one study researchers failed to fully inform participants that 'death anxiety' was the real focus of the study (Florian and Mikulincer, 1997).[1] A subsequent replication which provided fully informed consent obtained different findings (Tunnicliff 1998).

We have to return to the absolutist and relativist debate we first looked at in Chapter 1. If we take an absolute line on consent and deception then most psychological research is unethical. If we take a relativist line, then we might say that most psychological research falls within the ethical principles. The difficulty with the absolutist approach is that you prohibit virtually all psychological research. The difficulty with the relativist approach, on the other hand, is that you still have to draw a bottom line somewhere, so it cannot be used to allow *all* deception.

Confidentiality

The principle of confidentiality can pose some new ethical dilemmas of its own. What if you are carrying out some interviews and the participant, let's call her Binky, tells you that she has done a criminal act. Should you tell anyone and break confidentiality? This would contravene your ethical principles, but not reporting a crime goes against the general moral code of society. Maybe you would judge it on the nature of the crime. If Binky tells you she nicked some sweets from the pick 'n' mix when she was 8 then maybe that is OK. But what about if she tells you she burgled her elderly neighbour last week, or maybe that she likes using a chainsaw to cut up stray cats? It's not easy to make this decision. To disclose the information breaks your ethical principles, but to keep the confidence might lead to decimation of the local cat population.

Conclusion

Overall, we might suggest that the BPS principles are a thoughtful and interesting attempt to provide guidance for psychologists as they conduct their research. We will go on to look at some other ethical principles that might be considered, and then to look at how we might apply these principles to past and current research.

You are the president of the newly founded Psychological Society on the planet of Throg. The inhabitants of Throg have three brains, 27 legs and a keen sense of telepathy but a poor level of personal hygiene. You are given the task of drafting some new ethical guidelines. Suggest three important guidelines for the Throggies that will be different to the guidelines devised by humans.

Progress exercise

Limitations of ethical principles as a way of resolving ethical issues

The BPS principles offer guidance for psychologists when they carry out their research, but if we were putting a really critical eye on them what would we see as the limitations of this document? One issue to consider is whether there are any ethical principles that are missing or undervalued in the document.

What's missing?

Improving the quality of life

In Chapter 2 we suggested that: *the purpose of conducting any research is to establish knowledge that may be used to improve the world in which we live or to better understand ourselves and our behaviour.*

This aim is echoed by some psychologists and, most famously, George Miller (1969) in his presidential address to the American Psychological Association (APA) reminded us that the stated aim of the APA is to promote human welfare. He went on to consider what he meant by this phrase because it can be interpreted in different ways. One way to interpret it would be to argue for more control on our lives so that we are forced to behave better and hence improve our quality of life. If we had a Tab Patrol (the smoke police) to check out smokers and force them to quit then you might argue that our quality of life would be improved. However, many people might see Tab Patrol as an invasion on personal liberty and start muttering phrases like 'health fascists' and 'nanny state'. Miller's argument, was not to improve life by controlling people but that psychology can contribute to quality of life by encouraging a better understanding of ourselves so that we can be more aware of '*what is humanly possible and humanly desirable*'.

In Miller's view, we are all psychologists. Everyday we make judgements about our own behaviour and the behaviour of others. Just to engage in a casual conversation I have to have a model of what you are thinking and feeling and then match my words accordingly. Some psychology acknowledges this, but some psychology seeks to create an expert status for psychologists as people who know lots more about life and behaviour than ordinary people can ever hope to know. Miller does not buy into this and suggests: '*Our responsibility is less to assume the role of experts and try to apply psychology ourselves than to give it away to the people who really need it. . . .*'

Whatever view you take on the 'psychologist as expert' issue, you might well think that it is important for psychological research to make a useful contribution either to our knowledge or to the application of the subject. You might well suggest that there should be an additional ethical principle of *usefulness*, and that psychological research is required to demonstrate that it is making a contribution to improve the world we live in.

Racism

The BPS principles refer to issues of diversity but there is not a clear principle about inclusion, or respecting diversity. Racism, for example, is a social dilemma for each generation to wrestle with. Psychology has an uncomfortable past with race science and has sometimes provided a platform for racially offensive views. We would not deny that there might be some psychological questions to ask about race but there are so many scientific and political objections to this approach. In the first place we can only investigate racial differences if we can first define what race is and then carry out appropriate studies. As Jones (1991) points out, there are a number of problems including:

- the difficulty in defining race
- the history of social movement that has meant that many people have ancestors from many parts of the world
- within race variability is much greater than between race variability
- when comparative research is carried out, it has so far been impossible to obtain comparable samples of people from different races.

On the specific issue of IQ, the UK's only ever professor of psychometrics, Paul Kline, wrote:

> The only advantage in setting out the different scores on IQ tests of racial groups is to give ammunition to those who wish to decry them. It adds nothing to theoretical understanding or to social or educational practice. (Kline 1991: 96)

This analysis makes the enduring debate about racial differences all the more remarkable. You might hope that serious scientific and professional journals are careful and measured in their approach to this topic given its potential for mischief and harm. Unfortunately, this is not always the case and even the BPS in its professional journal *The Psychologist* chose to publish an article by academic controversialist Philippe Rushton (1990) which put forward an academically shallow but openly racist set of ideas. The article used evidence that was scientifically flawed to put forward a case for racial superiority of some races over others. The poor level of the science should have been enough to reject the article regardless of the unfounded conclusions that were being made.

We might reasonably suggest a further ethical principle of *anti-racism* whereby psychologists are asked to ensure that their work is not racist nor can it be used to cause racial offence.

Sexism

Women have had a difficult job being recognised in psychology. The content of psychology has largely been concerned with male behaviour and male experience, and academic psychology has created a number of barriers to the development and acceptance of its female colleagues. In the context of psychology, there has been a pervasive belittlement of women. If you look at the following quotes from famous male psychologists you will start to get the picture:

> We must start with the realisation that, as much as women want to be good scientists or engineers, they want first and foremost to be womanly companions of men and to be mothers. (Bruno Bettelheim 1965, cited in Weisstein 1992: 61)

> Much of a young woman's identity is already defined in her kind of attractiveness and in the selectivity of her search for the man (or men) by whom she wishes to be sought. . . . (Erik Erikson 1964, cited in Weisstein 1992: 62)

> Throughout history people have knocked their heads against the riddle of femininity. Nor will you have escaped worrying about this problem – those of you who are men; to those of you who

are women this will not apply – you are yourself the problem.
(Sigmund Freud 1973: 146; first published 1933)

These quotes are just a selection from a large sample of possible contributions. Women have been dealt generally by psychology either as a problem or as the nurturers of children and men. It is fair to say that women's voices are now louder in psychology than they were, but the body of knowledge that is used as psychological evidence still requires an analysis that highlights its gender bias.

It is worth noting how many of the classic studies in psychology were largely carried out on male subjects. For example, two of the most cited studies on prejudice, Sherif's (1956) study of conflict and competition and Tajfel's (1970) minimal group studies, were both carried out on boys. Kitzinger (1998) also points out that Erikson's model of identity across the lifespan is based on interviews with males, and Kohlberg's theory of moral development is based on a series of studies and interviews with males. We can argue for the inclusion of an ethical principle of *anti-sexism*, whereby psychologists seek to ensure that any bias or selectivity in their work is either acknowledged or reduced to a minimum.

We've picked out the two most written about 'isms' (racism and sexism), but clearly the list is endless. The general principle is that people should not be categorised and degraded because of the perceived group they belong to, whether it is their ethnicity, their sex, their age, their nationality, their appearance, their physical abilities, their scout troup, or whatever. This is a challenge for psychologists who commonly use typologies to categorise people or use visible variables such as ethnicity or sex to look for differences in whatever quality they are measuring. You might think it strange that issues of human respect like racism and sexism are not explicitly included in a statement of ethical behaviour, and you would not be alone in thinking that.

The uses of psychological research

Science cannot detach itself from everyday life. You might only be interested in your scientific project and have no interest in politics or other murky things like that, but if you end up inventing the *pocket nuclear disintegrator gun* (available in all good stores later this year) then this is not a good thing. It is unlikely that psychologists will invent a weapon of mass destruction, but they might well come up with theories or applications that will have a negative effect on large groups of people.

The apparently scientific issue of defining psychiatric conditions is a political battlefield. The decision to define a certain sort of behaviour as pathological can have a major effect on people's lives. The classification of homosexuality as a psychiatric condition in early versions of the *Diagnostic and Statistical Manual* (DSM) of the American Psychiatric Association led, not surprisingly, to very strong objections. More surprisingly those debates are still continuing. We will return to the controversial issue of diagnosis in Chapter 6.

Perhaps we can argue for an ethical principle to consider the *possible applications* of the research both positive and negative and to make efforts to reduce any of these possible negative uses.

Talking to the media

A professional hazard for psychologists is the insatiable thirst of the media for psychological analysis. On one level the information that psychologists give to media is an entertaining space-filler, but on another level it can have a major impact on the general public's view about events and about psychology. In the BPS Code of Conduct for Psychologists (2000) it says: *In all their work psychologists shall conduct themselves in a manner that does not bring into disrepute the discipline and the profession of psychology.*

We don't know about you, but the sight of psychologists on *Big Brother* commenting on whether Nush fancies whoever because of her body language makes us despair about psychology. Let's be clear about the limits of psychological knowledge. Psychologists cannot read thoughts and cannot read intentions. It is not part of our training and not part of our expertise. The comments on *Big Brother* and similar programmes can be seen as amusing nonsense, but they cannot be regarded as scientific analysis. I would therefore like to propose a further ethical principle of *don't talk b*ll*cks to the media*. With regard to *Big Brother* and similar shows there is probably very little harm in them (though you may have a different opinion), but there are other examples that we will consider in the next chapter which have far graver consequences.

The serious issue here is about giving the impression that you know more than you really do and speaking outside your level of expertise. Speaking confidently is a feature of many professional workers and my point here is that it is not right to intimidate the people you are working with by pretending to have expert knowledge which you do not have. With regard to non-verbal communication, much of the so-called analysis is carried out after the event so we interpret what a gesture meant, but is this ever put to the test? Is it really scientific knowledge or just pub-talk guesswork? If someone really could read body language then they could become a millionaire. They could go to the gambling tables and be able to read whether someone was bluffing or not. They don't go to the gambling tables and, in the same way that clairvoyants can never tell you the winner of the next race, they are claiming skills they do not have.

Using the principles and guidelines to judge research

Now that we have our principles, let's use them! Armed with my shield of ethical principles and my absolutist spear of truth, I can rip up virtually any piece of psychological research. This probably does not serve much real purpose but it might be useful in an essay when you are looking for an evaluative point. You need to be careful though. Let's have a look at the Milgram study. The details of this study commonly appear in introductory texts as the first example of unethical research. But is it?

Milgram was a good guy

If we go back to our four categories of ethics in Chapter 1 – consequences, actions, character and motive – then we might well argue that the *consequences* of Milgram's famous study are positive because it gives us a better understanding of evil and tyranny. His *motives* were sound because he was trying to answer questions about human behaviour raised by activities in World War II (1939–45), and we would say that he was a worthy *character* as evidenced by his writing and his other inventive and thought-provoking studies. The issue to consider is the *act* itself: the obedience study. If we look at our ethical principles and guidelines (above) then the important ones for this discussion are probably:

1. Consent
2. Deception
3. Debriefing
4. Withdrawal from the investigation
5. Confidentiality
6. Protection of participants.

On the issue of *consent*, you could argue that the participants consented to the procedure and, in fact, volunteered for it. They did not know what the point of it was but they chose to do what they did. They were able to *withdraw* and about a third of them did not complete the study. They were *debriefed* at the end of the study. They were *deceived* about the focus of the study but it would not have worked without that deception. They were also deceived about the nature of the electric shocks, in that the 'learner' was only pretending to be shocked. Mind you, this was probably a good thing as real shocks would have been more problematic (Milgram would have needed lots of confederates to be the 'learner').

The two issues that are harder to square are confidentiality and protection from harm. The *confidentiality* of some of the participants has been compromised by the film footage of the study, though we would hope that consent for showing that material was given at the time and is still sought each time the tape is reissued. On the issue of *protection from harm*, there is no doubt that the participants were subjected to an extremely stressful situation, and that some had strong physical responses to it. It is this charge that tends to hang around the study, and that, after the experimenters had witnessed a number of extreme stress responses, they could have chosen to terminate the study rather than continue it.

Milgram's defence was that he could not have known the outcome of the research before he started. Indeed, he asked psychiatrists how they expected people to behave in the study and they suggested that only a pathological minority would complete the study. Shows what they know! Milgram (cited in Colman 1987) further answered his critics by reporting the results of a follow-up survey of the subjects, carried out one year after the study. The results showed that 84 per cent said they were 'glad to have been in the experiment', and only 1.3 per cent said they were very sorry to have been in the experiment. Milgram also described how the subjects had been examined by a psychiatrist one year after the study who was unable to find one subject who showed signs of long-term harm. There is a good argument to be made that the cost-benefit sheet on this study comes down in favour of Milgram, because he did consider that he should stop the study:

> It became evident that some [subjects] would go to the end of the shock board, and some would experience stress. That point, it seems to me, is the first legitimate junction at which one could even start to abandon the study. But momentary excitement is not the same as harm. As the experiment progressed there was no indication of injurious effects on the subjects; and as the subjects themselves strongly endorsed the experiment, the judgment I made was to continue the investigation. (Milgram 1974: 212)

One final point to consider about the rights and wrongs of the Milgam study is that ethics are socially agreed rules. We noted in Chapter 1 that ethical principles vary with culture and time, so we can only judge people within the context of their culture and time. The ethical committee of the American Psychological Association investigated Milgram's research not long after the first publication and eventually came to the conclusion that it was ethically acceptable, though Milgram's membership was suspended while the committee deliberated the case. The American Association for the Advancement of Science awarded him a prize for outstanding contribution to social psychological research in 1965. In other words, Milgram's scientific peers considered the work and judged it to be ethical within their own criteria. So, by definition, Milgram's obedience study is ethical. We might not judge it the same way today, but it is not appropriate to judge Milgram badly when he was being accepted within the scientific community. If any judgement has to be made then it is against the whole scientific community and against psychology as an enterprise.

The prison simulation studies

Another famous study already mentioned in this text is Zimbardo's prison simulation carried out at Stanford University in 1971. This study paid students to play the part of either guard or prisoner in a make believe prison in the basement of the psychology department.

Zimbardo was aware of Milgram's research and the ethical issues it raised and therefore tried to deal with these issues by seeking informed consent and warning participants about the procedures he was undertaking. However, despite his care, the experiment had to be stopped by Zimbardo after six days because of the deteriorating state of the prisoners and the increasing level of abuse by the guards. That is Zimbardo's story anyway, though it is worth noting that his girlfriend at the time of the study, Christina Maslach (subsequently Zimbardo's wife and currently professor of psychology at University of California, Berkeley), went to see the study, was appalled at what she saw and ended up having a very big argument with Zimbardo. The study ended the next day (the power of love!).

Like the obedience studies of Milgram, this work has been subjected to sustained attack by psychologists about its ethical nature. In Chapter 2 we looked at the charge from Haslam and Reicher (2003) that Zimbardo effectively encouraged brutal behaviour by the guards, and we can add to that the issue of *protection from harm*, in that the prisoners were subjected to sustained degrading treatment. We can probably also raise issues of *consent* and *deception*, though like the obedience studies we might well be able to defend the experiment. The prison simulation has an extra and very damaging ethical problem, that of *withdrawal*.

There is video evidence of the prison simulation, though only a limited amount has ever been made available for public scrutiny by Zimbardo. On the bits available it is evident that the prisoners want to leave at one point. In fact one of the prisoners can be heard screaming 'I want out! I want out!' In another harrowing segment where the prisoners are engaged in a physical struggle with the guards, a prisoner can be heard screaming 'F*** the experiment and f*** Zimbardo!' while another voice screams 'It's a f****** simulation.' The viewer has a clear impression that the prisoners want to get out of the study and that they understand it is a role play. This goes against Zimbardo's interpretation that the prisoners internalised the prison and believed in it, and that even when given the opportunity to leave they did not. In fact, Zimbardo refused to let the prisoners out after this outburst and gave them the impression that they could not get out. Zimbardo argues that the roles of guard and prisoner are so powerful that they override human judgement and basic decency. In fact, Zimbardo subsequently argued that his experiment was so disturbing and unethical that it should not be replicated. The upside of this for Zimbardo was that his results and interpretation could not be challenged.

The charges against Zimbardo are that he did not pay enough attention to protecting his participants from *harm*, and that he did not allow them the opportunity to *withdraw* even when they screamed to be allowed out. He also seems to contravene some other principles that don't fit our list. First he took such an *active part* in the study that the result was contaminated by his own behaviour. You might argue that the behaviour in the prison was Zimbardo's creation. Second, by *misrepresenting* what went on and by arguing against any replication he gives a damaging and degrading picture of human behaviour.

This point is addressed by Haslam and Reicher (2003) when discussing their own prison simulation. They argue that Zimbardo's model of behaviour and stranglehold on the empirical data perpetuate an injustice in giving us such a negative and dispiriting view of human behaviour. They believed they had an intellectual responsibility to challenge the evidence and a moral and political responsibility to challenge his view of people. One of the big problems was how to carry out a prison simulation study that was ethical. The result of their efforts was *The Experiment*, a four-part series broadcast on BBC television in 2002.

This work is worth a book in itself but our interest here is with the ethics of the replication study and how Haslam and Reicher were able to satisfy psychology colleagues and the BBC of its ethical nature. You can read about this on the BBC website and also at the SEORG site at Exeter University (see end of chapter). The report of the independent ethics panel is comprehensive and persuasive. The panel was chaired by Lembit Opik, MP and the credentials of the others are impressive (you can download the whole ethics report to check this out). The brief of the panel was to ensure the welfare of all the participants. They reviewed the plans for the study, which included being allowed to stop the filming at any point. During the filming there was 24-hour para-medic and security guard cover. Two clinical psychologists were on set from 7.30am to 11.00pm every day and available on call at other times.

Without doubt it can be argued that every effort was made to protect the prisoners from *harm*. They were also made aware that they could *withdraw* at any time. The tricky issue here is one of *consent* because they could not have known what was going to happen or how they would deal with this novel situation. But, as argued about the obedience study, if we knew exactly what was going to happen there would be no point in doing the research. What did they find? Unfortunately there is not enough space in this text to describe the results of *The Experiment* (see a brief summary in Study Aids pages 144–5), though if we cut to the chase it provides a very strong challenge to Zimbardo's bleak picture of our behaviour.

Are we making a fuss about nothing?

Do we get too upset about ethics? Look at the way people are treated in the *Big Brother* house or humiliated on *Pop Idol* or some other reality television show. Surely it's OK to carry out psychology studies that wind people up a bit and trick them into unexpected behaviour? We would argue not, and although we accept that it is probably not helpful to take an absolutist position, it is important to consider the cost-benefits of any ethical violation. There needs to be some benefit from the study other than providing entertainment for psychologists and the general public.

Summary

The British Psychological Society has a statement of ethical principles and guidelines for research. These provide useful guidance for researchers and a useful tool for people who want to evaluate psychology. This list is not inclusive and it can be argued that other issues such as the racism, sexism and the uses of psychological research should also be considered. Looking back at some classic studies we can see that a robust argument can be made in defence of the Milgram obedience studies, though the Zimbardo prison simulation, in the opinion of the authors, is much harder to defend. Haslam and Reicher have shown that it is possible to carry out challenging studies within the bounds of ethical principles. But hey kids, don't do this at home!

Further reading

Colman, A. (1987) *Facts, Fallacies and Frauds in Psychology*, London: HarperCollins.

Miller, G. (1969) Psychology as a means of promoting human welfare, *American Psychologist* 24, 1063–75.

Richards, G. (1998) The case of psychology and 'race', *The Psychologist* 11, 179–81.

Websites

SEORG The Experiment (Haslam and Reicher) <www.ex.ac.uk/Psychology/seorg/exp/> <http://news.bbc.co.uk/1/hi/entertainment/tv_and_radio/1779816.stm>

Milgram's research is discussed on many websites, such as <www.stanleymilgram.com/> or <www.stanleymilgram.com/references.html>

Details of Zimbardo's research can be found on <www.prisonexp.org/> (Stanford Prison Study, 81 slides of the experiment) and <www.stanford.edu/dept/news/relaged/970108prisonexp.html> (discussion of the lessons and ethical issues raised by the prison experiment).

British Psychological Society and ethics <www.bps.org.uk/about/rules5.cfm>

Ethical issues in different kinds of research

This chapter looks at the range of methods that psychologists use to gather data and gives some examples of ethical issues that each method poses. Much of the research that we have discussed has taken place in a laboratory setting and been experimental. In fact many people equate laboratory experiments with unethical practices. A scrubbed laboratory seems a place of potential torture, where the subject/participant is at the mercy of the experimenter. However, other kinds of research are also prone to ethical problems.

Experiments

Field experiments

In some field experiments, which are conducted outside the laboratory, participants are not aware that they are taking part in an experiment. An **independent variable** (IV) is manipulated and a **dependent variable** (DV) is measured, but the setting is more naturalistic than a

ETHICAL ISSUES AND GUIDELINES IN PSYCHOLOGY

laboratory experiment. For example, in one field experiment referred to previously on the effects of perceived authority on obedience, confederates dressed in a sports jacket and tie, a milkman's uniform, or as a guard, and made requests to passersby, for example, asking them to pick up some litter or to give someone a dime for the parking meter (Bickman 1974). In this study the IV was the clothes worn by the confederate and the DV was willingness to obey the request. (Incidentally, participants obeyed most when the confederate was dressed as a guard.)

In general field experiments are conducted in more natural environments. Another key feature is that in most field experiments (or any field study) participants are less likely to respond to any **demand characteristics** or **experimenter bias** because *they probably don't know that their behaviour is being recorded*. It can be argued that this disregards their right to privacy and right to autonomy and respect. A well-known example is the 'Good Samaritan' field study by Piliavin *et al.* (1969). Psychology students boarded subway trains in New York city with the aim of seeing how passengers would respond to an emergency situation. A confederate faked some kind of collapse (either holding a bottle and smelling of alcohol or using a cane). The student observers made note of how long it took for help to be forthcoming.

What are the ethical issues here? There was no possibility of gaining prior consent, nor was it possible after the experiment to inform people about the study. This challenges the participants' right to autonomy. In addition participants might have experienced some psychological distress either from what they witnessed or their own feelings of self-doubt because they didn't help. There would have been no opportunity to reassure them afterwards.

There is also the issue of privacy. A general rule (as we will see later) is that people should not be observed in a study unless it is in a public place; in other words one where it is usual to be observed by others. The subway setting would then not count as an invasion of privacy. According to this rule, the Good Samaritan study would be acceptable and arguably the Tearoom Trade study (see page 27) might be OK too because it is usual to be observed by a watchqueen (there are other ethical objections to this study). Would it be acceptable to observe lovers on a park bench?

The three ethical issues (consent, harm, privacy) discussed so far relate to participants' rights. Kimmel (1996) also points out that there are wider issues for the profession and society. Once such studies become general knowledge (and a number of psychological studies do make their way into the popular press), then people start to think that a person collapsing on the underground could just be a confederate in a psychology experiment. Such deceptions bring psychology into disrepute and may alter the behaviour of the general public.

At their best, these studies give us an insight into how people behave in everyday situations, at their worst they are little more than a 'candid camera' technique[1] used to wind people up and then chuckle at their response. (*I believe that* 'You've Been Framed' *still pays £250 for each tape if you're interested – ed*).

Natural experiments

There are situations where it would be impossible to manipulate an independent variable but such 'manipulation' occurs naturally; for example, exposing individuals to television and observing what effect this has on their behaviour. The problem is that there are not many people who have never watched television. There are, however, some communities where television has only recently been introduced, such as St Helena (an island in the middle of the South Atlantic Ocean). This gives psychologists the natural opportunity to observe the effects of television (the independent variable) on, for example, antisocial behaviour (a dependent variable; Charlton *et al.* 2000).

What ethical issues arise from such research? It is usually possible to gain informed consent from participants but there are new problems. In the St Helena study the presence of psychologists studying the community may have been intrusive and altered the behaviour of participants. This could be seen as a form of psychological harm.

Privacy is also an issue with natural experiments, as with other kinds of research. Simply removing the names of individuals may be insufficient to ensure privacy as other details may identify the locality where the research took place, as in the case of the research on St Helena. In such a study community members may easily be able to identify individuals.

Another important issue with this style of research is to consider whether the naturally occurring variable is an important one, whether the results tell us anything worthwhile and whether the research is socially sensitive. One of the most obvious and commonly researched natural variables[2] is what sex you are – male or female. There are numerous studies that compare the average performance of men and women on a variety of measures. If you take the average score of men on some dimension and compare it with the average score of women you commonly find a small difference. However, the spread of scores *within* men and women far outweighs the *difference* between the two groups. Also with regard to sex differences in children, for example, reviews of the research into cognitive ability and social behaviour have consistently found that there are very few measurable differences, and in the cases where there is a difference the effect is very small (for example, Woolley 1910, cited in Williams 1987; Maccoby and Jacklin 1974).

Look at the example distributions in Figure 4.1. They show the different distributions of boys and girls on a made up variable of 'binkiness'. You will see that girls have an average binkiness score a little higher than boys, but that the distributions overlap so much that it would be impossible to predict a person's binkiness score just by knowing their sex. An analysis of research on the development of social and cognitive behaviour found that male–female difference accounted for only 1 to 5 per cent of the variance in the population (Deaux 1984). This means that sex is a very poor predictor of how an individual will behave.

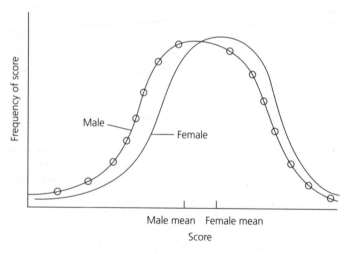

Figure 4.1 **Distributions of binkiness in males and females**

The ethical problem here is that by using the easy-to-measure variable of sex, the researchers tend to exaggerate the importance of that variable and give an unrealistic picture of how people can and do behave. The same can also be said for the even more controversial variable of race. You can put these examples under the heading of socially sensitive research. Conclusions are reached which may not be valid; for example, concluding that there are significant differences between men and women when the differences between the two sexes are very small in comparison to the differences within the sexes. It is 'socially sensitive' because such research has a social impact; in other words research that may affect people's lives. The issue of socially sensitive research is discussed in Chapter 5.

Laboratory experiments

As we have seen, in some experiments it may be necessary to deceive participants. Some experimenters have sought ways round this, as we will see later, but have still faced accusations of unethical practice. In Zimbardo's (1973) 'mock prison' study participants were informed prior to the study about what would be involved – namely that they would be assigned the role of prisoner or guard and then required to act out the designated role. In order to enhance the realism of the study, Zimbardo arranged for the 'prisoners' to be 'arrested' by the police in their own homes. It is debatable about whether this counts as deception. The participants gave their voluntary consent to take part in the study but were not fully informed about key events that would take place.[3] It is probably unrealistic to expect participants to be informed about everything as long as they are informed about any factors that may influence their decision to take part. The 'home arrest' information may not ultimately have mattered to any participants.

In another study of social influence, Gamson *et al.* (1982) tried to circumvent the problem of deception by arranging for participants to agree to be deceived. The researchers advertised for participants and when interested individuals telephoned they were asked whether they were willing to participate in any or all of the following kinds of research:

1. Research on brand recognition of commercial products.
2. Research on product safety.

3. Research in which you will be misled about the purpose until afterwards.
4. Research involving group standards.

Most people said yes to all four and were then told that only the last kind of research was in progress. However, they had agreed to the third kind of research and thus consented to be deceived probably without really being aware of it. Were they still deceived?

The study itself involved the groups of nine participants being asked to take part in a discussion which would be videotaped and used by a (fictitious) public relations firm, MHRC. The PR company wanted the group to say what they thought about a Mr C who ran a petrol station for an oil company. He had been fired because of immoral behaviour and was now suing the oil company. The co-ordinator instructed individuals to argue as if they were offended by Mr C's behaviour. The groups soon realised that they were being manipulated to produce a tape of evidence supporting the oil company's position. This led to further discussion about whether to give permission for the videotapes to be used (three-quarters of the groups declined to give their consent).

Afterwards, many of the participants reported feelings of anxiety and stress. One said, 'I'm glad to have done it but I'm really shook up and my blood pressure will be high for hours.' Another called the experiment 'the most stressful experience I've had in the past year'. The researchers recognised their moral obligations and stopped the study before it was completed, but nevertheless participants had clearly been subjected to psychological distress. This may influence our judgement about the initial deception – people find deception acceptable when the task is relatively harmless (see Christiansen 1988).

Non-experimental research

Observational studies

We have already considered an observational study (the 'tearoom trade') in which there was disregard for privacy and in which no consent was possible. As we have already noted, observing anyone in a public place may appear to be acceptable but it may also be important to consider what behaviours are being observed. For example, people may not think it an invasion of privacy to be observed in a park on a sunny day but might object if the observers' aim was to record instances of sexual activity (as in Humphreys' study).

Some researchers have been interested in casual conversations. The obvious way to study this is to listen in on other people's conversations. Moore (1922) spent weeks walking round New York, writing down everything he heard and uncovering some interesting exchanges. In a more recent study Levin and Arluke (1985) made their record more impersonal by simply recording tone and focus. How would you feel if you found out that one of these studies had listened in to your conversation? Would you feel that this was an invasion of privacy? Would you like to do the study yourself? Don't you do this as an amateur psychologist most days? Is there a difference between a formal study and informal observations?

A classic study by Festinger *et al.* (1956) involved participant observation, a technique where the observer is also a participant in the action. The aim of this study was to see how a group of people would respond when they found their beliefs threatened. A certain Mrs. Keech had a small but loyal following for her unusual religious beliefs. She predicted that the world was going to end on a certain day and gathered believers around her to witness the end of the world. Festinger and colleagues infiltrated the group to see what happened. The world didn't end and those present concluded that their faith had saved the world. There is little doubt that those present would have felt horrified if they knew there were imposters present and even more aggrieved if they knew the reason why. Of course other questions arise about how much the psychologists took part in the group activity and encouraged the behaviour of Mrs. Keech. Did they in fact incite much of her behaviour?

In the above studies the observations were **undisclosed**. In other words the individuals had no awareness that they were being watched or listened to and did not know that such observations would be used for research purposes. In some studies observations are **disclosed**, for example, Ainsworth *et al.*'s (1974) study of infant behaviour in the Strange Situation. The intention of this study was to observe the level of distress shown by a child when it was left on its own by its caregiver so that they could assess the type of attachment between caregiver and child. There has never been any suggestion of long-term psychological harm arising from this study but you don't have to be a rocket scientist to realise that there were a lot of tears.

Cross-cultural research

Cross-cultural research has given us a rich source of data about diverse groups of people and how they live. At its best it enhances our understanding and gives dignity to people who sometimes do not have a voice. As ever though, not all examples of this research reach the highest levels of good practice and there are some ethical issues to deal with. Cross-cultural research is commonly conducted by western psychologists and they bring to their research their own views of life and how it should be lived. It is impossible to be free from bias so it is inevitable that some part of the researcher's views intrude into the observations made of people.

In addition the use of techniques developed in one culture and used in another (called **imposed etics**) may mean comparisons made between cultural groups are not valid. For example, intelligence tests that were written and trialled with North American students may not be a fair test of intelligence among South Americans. To draw cross-cultural conclusions about intelligence using such tests may unfairly portray other cultures as inferior. This is an ethical issue and also an example of socially sensitive research.

Another example can be seen in the work of Lawrence Kohlberg on moral development. He devised some moral dilemmas that draw out how people make decisions of right and wrong. He used these dilemmas in many parts of the world and found that the children of different countries gave different responses to these dilemmas. He concluded that the most morally developed children in the world were American children from urban environments. He did not appear to take account of the fact that the dilemmas were devised in an urban American environment (Colby and Kohlberg 1987).

In addition, it has been argued (Nobles 1976) that western researchers have plundered African people for knowledge and information in much the same way as economic colonists plundered raw materials. Nobles argues that the data and knowledge should belong to people who are the source of it. This would match up with the idea of seeing people as participants rather than subjects.

Questionnaire

Questionnaire studies are very commonly used today because of the speed of collecting data and their relative ease of analysis and comparison. It is estimated that about one third of all data in British psychology journals comes from questionnaire studies (Banyard and Hunt 2000). The most common way to collect this data is through handing out survey forms to students, often at the start of a lecture. It is not clear how much the student is being coerced to take part (in the USA such studies often form part of college course requirements), so there are sometimes issues of consent to consider. The questionnaire might also contain questions that could offend or cause distress. This also has to be considered when reviewing the research.

A further ethical issue, in relation to questionnaire surveys, is how the data from the survey is used. This issue will be discussed in detail in the chapter on socially sensitive research.

Research using correlational analysis

We often want to know the *cause* of events or behaviour. Why did that happen, or why did you behave like that? We want reasons and causes. Experiments allow us to make inferences about what caused something because we have manipulated the variables (or they have been naturally manipulated) and found out what effect they have. Correlational analysis, on the other hand, does not involve any manipulation and therefore we commonly say that we cannot infer cause from correlational data. This goes against our intuition and so we probably accept that smoking cigarettes causes cancer even though the evidence is correlational rather than experimental. To test this relationship experimentally we would have to take a number of non-smokers and randonly assign them to smoking and non-smoking groups and come back in 20 years to see how many have developed cancer. As this research idea would never be acceptable we are stuck with correlational studies on such topics. The problem with the correlational evidence on smoking is that people who choose to smoke might be different from the people who choose not to smoke. In fact work by H.J. Eysenck (1991) (sponsored not surprisingly by the tobacco companies) found that if you remove differences in stress from the data then the cancer rates of smokers and non-smokers are *not* significantly different.

We intuitively believe in the coincidence of events. If two things happen together we tend to believe they are causally related. Just look at all the possible medicines and remedies there are on the market for all manner of health problems. Most health problems and psychiatric problems get better by themselves given enough time, but if you take a remedy (for example, Banyard and Flanagan's Magic Elixir of Life™, only 3 instalments of £29.99 gets you a month's supply) then we can guarantee that most people will get better if they take it for a few weeks whatever they have wrong with them. Many might come to believe that the Magic Elixir of Life™ is, in fact, magic and buy loads more of it. The real magic is most likely to be the way that our bodies can heal us without us having to do anything. Mind you, we won't point that out because that would be bad for business and bad for all our fellow travellers on the untested and unproved medicine circuit: stand up homeopaths, acupuncturists, counsellors and astrologers.[4] In case you think that comment is harsh then try looking for controlled studies on the effectiveness of any of those therapies.

The ethical issues that arise with correlational analyses come in the failure fully to explain the nature of the evidence. People have a tendency to attribute causal explanations to information that does not support these attributions (Heider 1958), and researchers could be clearer about the limitations of their findings.

Having said that, the issue of causation is much more complicated than the simple distinction between the logic of experiments and correlations. Very little applied psychology is able to use experimental methods and commonly relies on regression analysis (a statistical technique whereby relationships between variables can be calculated). Although this analysis does not allow us to make statements about what causes what, it does allow us to use our data to predict events and sometimes behaviour. So, for example with the smoking data, we cannot say that smoking *causes* lung cancer and heart disease, but we can say that if you smoke there is *an increased probability* that you will get lung cancer or heart disease in later life. In other words we can use the data about smoking to predict illness.

Summary

Ethical problems are not confined to laboratory experiments in psychology. The common stereotype of the laboratory experiment as being ethically dubious and all other methods being ethically sound is incorrect. Every data collection technique and every location presents its own ethical challenges, and it is necessary to return to the principles of good practice when conducting any research.

Further reading

Francis, R.D. (1999) *Ethics for Psychologists: A Handbook*. Leicester: BPS Books.

Websites

The St Helena website gives information research about the island. <http://website.lineone.net/~sthelena/> Alternatively you can try Gloucester University's site <www.glos.ac.uk/education/content.asp?sid=4>

If you want to take a sceptical look at incredible scientific claims then go to

5

Socially sensitive research

 Socially sensitive issues
Should socially sensitive research be avoided?
How should psychologists conduct socially sensitive research?
Summary

This chapter is about research that has a direct effect on individual people or on society in general. You might argue that all psychology has such an effect, and if it doesn't then what's the point? Everything is a matter of degree though, and in this chapter we are concerned with research that might damage people or which may have an impact on general attitudes, and there's plenty of it to discuss. Important issues are often sensitive issues and that is what makes them important. It is not surprising, therefore, that psychologists sometimes upset or challenge people. The issue of child sexual abuse is about as sensitive and distressing a topic as you can imagine, but it is important to research the area so that abuse can be reduced or prevented and the victims can be helped. This research is likely to be sensitive and distressing to the participants, the researchers and also to those who have to deal with the findings from such research. It has key implications for social policy. In this chapter we will look at what we mean by socially sensitive issues, at the decision about whether or not to conduct such research and finally at how such research can be conducted.

Socially sensitive issues

How can we define a 'socially sensitive issue'? As individuals we are sensitive to a wide range of texts, issues and images. On the relatively simple issue of displaying parts of your body in public, some people are grossly offended by even minor displays of flesh and other people 'get their kit off' at the slightest suggestion. One person's offence is another person's 'bit of a laugh'.

There are many definitions of what constitutes a sensitive topic, though the most commonly cited is by Sieber and Stanley who define socially sensitive research as: *'Studies in which there are potential consequences or implications, either directly for the participants in the research or for the class of individuals represented by the research'* (1988: 49). This definition is very broad and allows the inclusion of topics that are not commonly thought of as sensitive, such as research on the smoking habits of children. It also alerts psychologists to their responsibilities to wider society. One criticism made of this definition is that it may lead us to equate social sensitivity with 'controversial'. Renzetti and Lee (1993) suggest that an alternative is to define socially sensitive topics as those that seem either threatening or contain an element of risk in some way. Such research involves potential costs and consequent problems for both the participants and researchers. Lee (1993) suggests there are three issues that create a concern about sensitivity. The first of these issues are those considered *private, stressful, or sacred*, such as sexuality or death. The second are those issues that if revealed might cause *stigmatisation or fear*, such as studies that reveal illegal behaviour. The final issues are related to the presence of a *political threat* where researchers may study areas subject to controversy or social conflict.

Examples of socially sensitive research

A recent piece of research into the behaviour of gay men reported that some men were trying to infect themselves with AIDS (www. nyaidscoalition.org 2003). This behaviour has been referred to as bug chasing. The research considered the complex motivations for this behaviour but was criticised because it portrayed a negative image of gay men. The argument here is that the general public are likely to generalise to all gay men from the unusual examples of a few. There was no question about the quality of the research, only whether people should be told about it. The dilemma here for researchers is whether to report what they find or whether to be more concerned with how the wider group is viewed.

Research on the prevalence of smoking, alcohol abuse or drug use is sensitive because such activities may be illegal. If information is sought from underage smokers or drinkers then parental permission may be needed and this may prevent teenagers from being willing to take part.

A different example is research on domestic violence; for example, interviews with those who have been abused to determine the effects of such violence or surveys of how frequently such episodes take place (husbands being violent to their wives or children, and wives being abusive towards their husbands). Research on domestic abuse investigates topics that are private and stressful and therefore have the potential to cause further pain and harm to individuals who are already experiencing abuse. It may also expose incriminating information and expose individuals to risk. Researchers need to be fully prepared to deal with the likely effects of the research; for example, the effects on participants, on their families, on the researchers themselves (conducting such research may be distressing) and on the implications of the research for legislation.

Another example of a sensitive issue is the false memory/recovered memory debate (see also Chapter 2). Over the past 20 years the famous memory psychologist Elizabeth Loftus has written about the validity of 'recovered memories' of childhood abuse. These memories commonly come to light only after therapeutic sessions with people who use techniques such as guided imagery to explore early life experiences. Until the therapy, the clients had been unaware of any abuse as a child. Loftus's work with experimental memory studies as well as through legal work has led her to argue that even though these 'memories' appear to be very believable, they are often the result of recent reconstructive processes rather than of past events. This research is socially sensitive because there are potential consequences for people who have claimed to have recovered memories and for their families.

A commonly cited example of socially sensitive research is research related to IQ, especially the links made between intelligence and race. An example of such research is a study by Jensen (1969) where he argued that the reason for the 15-point IQ difference between Black and White Americans was basically due to genetic rather than environmental differences. This research sparked off a lasting emotional and political controversy. Such research has innumerable social and personal consequences; for example, one explanation as to why Black Americans have lower IQs is because they have lower expectations about how they are likely to perform – expectations created in part by IQ research. Psychology has a long history of being associated with race science[1] which has sought to categorise people on the basis of their physical characteristics and look for cognitive and behavioural differences. As mentioned earlier in this text in relation to the intelligence debate, this enterprise is scientifically flawed and socially divisive (in the authors' view) because it emphasises minor or non-existent differences between ethnic groups rather than the many values and behaviours and ambitions that they share. This is not to say that there are no scientific questions to ask about this issue, but if it is virtually impossible to define race (Jones 1991; see Chapter 2 in this text) and very difficult to find comparable samples in different cultures then the conclusions drawn from the research will be open to much question and debate.

We would argue that the teaching of socially sensitive issues like anorexia can also raise serious ethical issues. If we are to believe the research into anorexia then it is likely that teachers deal every day with students who have such eating disorders. Anorexia nervosa is estimated to affect as many as 1 in 100 people (Matlin 1987), though estimates of young women with mild versions of the disorder are as high as 10 per cent (Brownell and Foreyt 1986). Around 15 per cent of women who are diagnosed as having anorexia nervosa die from the disorder and under half regain a reasonable adjustment to eating. Teachers might well know the theory of eating disorders but are unlikely to be trained as counsellors to deal with the response they may get from vulnerable students. The problem is made worse by the expectation of many students that their psychology teacher has professional counselling skills as well as teaching skills.

1. Consider how each of the main ethical guidelines applies in particular to socially sensitive research. For example, you might consider how informed consent, deception, privacy, confidentiality and protection from physical and psychological harm are all issues in named pieces of socially sensitive psychological research.
2. Select one socially sensitive study and present arguments about the costs and benefits (consider costs/benefits to participants, researchers, people who may be affected by the findings and society in general).

Cultural sensitivity

All research requires 'cultural sensitivity': the understanding that enables us to gain access to individuals in society, to learn about their lifestyles and to communicate in ways that the individuals understand, believe, regard as relevant to themselves and are likely to act upon. Sieber argues:

> Cultural sensitivity has nothing to do with the art and music of a culture, and almost everything to do with respect, shared decision making and effective communication. Too often, researchers ignore the values, the life-style and the cognitive and affective world of the subjects. They impose their own, perhaps in an attempt to reform people whose culture they would like to eradicate, or perhaps simply out of ignorance about the subjects' reality. (Sieber 1992: 129)

Being sensitive to other cultures is easier said than done. We are all affected by the bias of **ethnocentrism**. In our everyday lives we are asked to make judgements about people and events. We have a range of opinions that we are prepared to offer to other people when asked, and sometimes when not asked. In our judgements we are often inclined to show a little egocentrism (seeing things from our own particular viewpoint to the exclusion of others) or show ethnocentrism (seeing things from the point of view of our group). Ethnocentrism can be defined as the following syndrome of behaviours (LeVine and Campbell 1972):

- a tendency to under-value the out-group's products
- an increased rejection and hostility towards out-group members
- a tendency to over-value the in-group's products
- an increased liking for in-group members (accompanied by pressures for conformity and group cohesion).

With an ethnocentric standpoint we tend to see our own group as being best. Also, we underestimate the errors and failings in our own team and exaggerate them in the opposing team. There are a number of reasons for this, including our access to evidence. We observe the behaviour of people like ourselves because we mix with them, but we do not appear to mix outside our own groups very much. Recent reports (Ouseley 2001; Guardian 2004) suggest that school playgrounds are becoming more segregated by ethnicity as children prefer the company of children from their own cultural communities. We are likely to know far more about the behaviour and opinions of people we mix with and people who are like us. Also, if we support people like ourselves then we are likely to receive support back from these people. We expect our friends to support us and not to do us down, particularly in the company of strangers. It is all to do with social cohesion and a sense of belonging. The downside of the ethnocentric outlook is that we are likely to show *prejudice* towards people who are not like us and not in our group.

How does ethnocentrism intrude into psychology? Ethnocentrism means that we give undue prominence to our own group of people. An analysis of introductory textbooks (Smith and Bond 1993) found that they mainly cited work by US researchers. In a fairly standard US text by Baron and Byrne (1991) 94 per cent of the 1700 studies mentioned were in fact from the USA. In a British text (Hewstone *et al.* 1988), about 66 per cent of the studies were American, 32 per cent were European and under 2 per cent came from the rest of the world. These books are by no means exceptional and reflect the places where psychological research is conducted. It is estimated by Rosenzweig (1992, cited in Smith and Bond 1993) that there are 56,000 psychology researchers in the world and about 64 per cent of them are American.

So, psychological research is mainly conducted by Americans and Europeans and they mainly study themselves. This means that the psychology in our textbooks is the psychology of Americans and Europeans, but it is by no means clear whether the behaviour these people display is the same behaviour we can expect in other cultures and other lifestyles. This means we have two possible sources of bias: (a) researchers mainly study their own culture; (b) researchers find it difficult to interpret the behaviour and experience of people from other cultures. The issue is even more complex than that because within British and American culture there are a range of ethnically diverse peoples, not all of whom are represented with psychology.

Should socially sensitive research be avoided?

Many psychologists might feel that they would prefer to avoid difficult and sensitive work for fear of getting it wrong. As a result, vulnerable and distressed people might not receive valuable support. But if you offer that support and get it badly wrong you might end up doing more harm than good. It's a tough call.

So, where does this leave us? Well if you want an easy life, don't do socially sensitive research. An APA report (2001) noted that institutional review boards (similar to ethical committees) were twice as likely to reject socially sensitive proposals. Non-sensitive proposals that did not include ethical problems were approved 95 per cent of the time, but comparable sensitive ones were approved only about 50 per cent of the time. The same statistics were reported by Ceci *et al.* (1985), which suggests that despite increased awareness of the importance of socially sensitive research it is still being avoided. Sieber and Stanley (1988: 55) advised against this:

Sensitive research addresses some of society's pressing social issues and policy questions. Although ignoring the ethical issues in sensitive research is not a responsible approach to science, shying away from controversial topics, simply because they are controversial, is also an avoidance of responsibility.

Many psychologists do recognise that they must bite the bullet. For example, Liebling and Shah (2001) conducted a sensitive study on the abuse of women and children during the civil war in Uganda. They wrote in their introduction to the report:

We argue that although important consideration should be given to cultural sensitivities, and the support and safety of all those involved when conducting such research, this should not be at the expense of the prevalent continued silence surrounding abuse of women and children.

The APA report (2001) also notes that psychologists do in fact take importance into account when deciding whether research should or should not be conducted. This was shown in a study where researchers were asked to judge pairs of deliberately flawed experiments that were identical except for the importance of their subject matter. The researchers who were questioned were significantly more likely to overlook methodological problems and to recommend publication when they perceived the topic to be important.

How should psychologists conduct socially sensitive research?

If we believe that socially sensitive research should be conducted (though you may not agree with this), the next step is to establish principles for conducting such research. Sieber and Stanley (1988) wrote their important article to make just this point: that psychological codes of conduct offer little guidance about how to resolve the ethical questions raised by socially sensitive research, which is an important omission. Their recommendation was not to take the path of resolving the problem by not doing it, but to work out some principles to guide such research. More recently Sieber (2005) argued that 'actual sensitivity is present more in the social context of the research than the topic'. In other words the focus of psychologists should be more on what they do rather than what topics should or should not be investigated. We will consider a few suggestions for dealing with the especial problems raised in socially sensitive research.

Sampling

Often socially sensitive research focuses on groups of people who have to be selected using special sampling methods. For example, conducting research on domestic violence is best done by interviewing people who have had such experiences rather than asking a general sample and obtaining a very small number of respondents who have anything relevant to say. One way to do this is to start with a few people who are known to have experienced abuse and ask them for the names of other people they know who have had similar experiences. This is called the *snowball sampling* technique. Sieber (1992) points out that potential participants may feel uncomfortable with a direct approach so it is preferable to contact these people in such a way that they can easily refuse to take part; for example, by sending a letter describing the study and the measures that will be taken to protect confidentiality. An alternative strategy would be to use an advertisement with a phone number connected to an answering machine or post office box (Parker and Ulrich 1990). Whilst public recruitment may increase the number of interviewees, there are associated risks with this strategy that should be evaluated carefully in relation to the phenomenon under investigation.

Interviewing techniques

One of the ethical issues that can arise with socially sensitive research is that the participants might be vulnerable and distressed or might have a number of unresolved conflicts, and therefore might not be fully in control of the interview. In the research process the skilled researcher may extract more information from the participant than she or he intended to disclose (Sieber and Stanley 1988). The interviewer may have developed his or her skills over a number of years and know how to get to the heart of the story, and the participant may be disclosing this information for the first time so will not have rehearsed the story or thought through the implications of telling it. Interviewers therefore should be especially aware of the potential for extracting more information than the respondent may wish to reveal. Careful training is very important.

Confidentiality

Participants in socially sensitive research may experience threats to their physical and psychological safety as a consequence of their involvement in research. It may not be sufficient to protect confidentiality by withholding names as individuals may still be identifiable. This means that the potential consequences of exposure must be weighed carefully at the outset against the potential benefits. A cost-benefit analysis is one way of dealing with ethical issues. One of the benefits of socially sensitive research is that participants may gain from the opportunity to discuss their problems. For example, an interviewee during research into the experience of domestic violence made the following comment: 'Being interviewed by you was more useful than the counsellors at X' (McCosker *et al*. 2001).

Wider responsibilities

A key aspect of socially sensitive research is the consequences that it has for the wider community, not just the specific participants. For example, research on black Americans may have effects on how all black Americans are treated, which may be a positive or a negative effect. Sieber (2005) suggests that members of the wider community are consulted during the planning phase of a research study and their views should be sought before a final report is produced. Individual participants should also have an opportunity to comment on the final report before publication.

Dealing with cultural sensitivity

In terms of cultural sensitivity the American Psychological Association has published an extensive set of guidelines on multicultural research (APA 2002). These are shown in Box 5.1. In the background material to this set of guidelines they note that the profession of psychology in the USA is not representative of all peoples. Around 67 per cent of the total population describe themselves as white with the biggest other cultural groups being African-American and Hispanic, each of which account for 13 per cent of the population. In psychology, however, if you look at the people obtaining a first degrees in psychology then only 10 per cent are African-American and 10 per cent are Hispanic. When it comes to doctorates then the figure for these two minority groups drops to 5 per cent, and membership of the APA is only 2.1 per cent Hispanic and 1.7 per cent African-American.

Psychology can contribute to our understanding of people from different backgrounds to ourselves. It can add to our personal cultural sensitivity, but it can also contribute to cultural misunderstandings.

Box 5.1 Guidelines on Multicultural Education, Training, Research, Practice, and Organizational Change for Psychologists (APA 2002)

Guideline #1: Psychologists are encouraged to recognize that, as cultural beings, they may hold attitudes and beliefs that can detrimentally influence their perceptions of and interactions with individuals who are ethnically and racially different from themselves.

Guideline #2: Psychologists are encouraged to recognize the importance of multicultural sensitivity/responsiveness, knowledge, and understanding about ethnically and racially different individuals.

Guideline #3: As educators, psychologists are encouraged to employ the constructs of multiculturalism and diversity in psychological education.

Guideline #4: Culturally sensitive psychological researchers are encouraged to recognize the importance of conducting culture–centered and ethical psychological research among persons from ethnic, linguistic, and racial minority backgrounds.

Guideline #5: Psychologists strive to apply culturally–appropriate skills in clinical and other applied psychological practices.

Guideline #6: Psychologists are encouraged to use organizational change processes to support culturally informed organizational policy.

Summary

When it comes down to it virtually all psychological research is socially sensitive so the message is that in all psychological research the researchers should be aware of the social consequences of what they do. However, some research is especially sensitive for the participants, for their wider community and for social policy. In this chapter we have looked at some examples of socially sensitive research, such as that with homosexual groups, victims of domestic violence, IQ and people with eating disorders. The delicate nature of such research has led researchers and ethical committees to avoid conducting studies in these areas. However not conducting socially sensitive research is also argued to be undesirable. Thus we must seek ways of dealing with the issues that arise. This includes simply being aware of the problems that may arise and weighing costs against benefits.

Further reading

Sieber, J.E. and Stanley, B. (1988) Ethical and professional dimensions of socially sensitive research, *American Psychologist*, 43(1), 49–55. (The original article that sparked off much of the thinking on socially sensitive research, discusses the issues as well as ways of dealing with them.)

Websites

APA guidelines on multicultural research <www.apa.org/pi/multiculturalguidelines/>

6

Psychology in practice

Military psychology
The conduct of psychologists
Speaking out
Summary

This chapter looks at some of the ethical dilemmas that arise with the practice of psychology. We have chosen our examples to give you a flavour of the work that psychologists do and the dilemmas they encounter. We start with military psychology, and move on to the conduct of psychologists in the media and in therapeutic situations and how they choose to speak out or stay silent about important issues. The health warning that goes with this chapter says that we have chosen a number of controversial examples to make our points and we hope you don't end up with the impression that all psychologists are scurrilous disreputable charlatans.

Military psychology

A major area of research for psychologists that raises serious issues is military psychology. The ethics of warfare are difficult to unravel. If you are a pacifist and would never use violence and believe we should not use weapons against other human beings then the moral issue is clear – fighting is wrong. Many people, however, would be prepared to fight or even use weapons in certain circumstances; for example, to protect themselves, or to protect their family and friends or even their property. They might be prepared to fight for a cause and they might believe that some military acts are morally justified. Whatever you believe, it is clear that armies and warfare have been a major influence on the development of human societies and continue to be so. Thousands of men and women in this country and abroad are employed by military forces and millions are affected by military actions.

Psychology has been involved with the military for over a hundred years and its involvement raises a number of ethical issues. The most fundamental of these is whether you believe it is right to help a military organisation become more efficient. If you are a pacifist then the answer is obviously no, but if you accept the need for an army then it makes sense to use all the resources at your disposal including psychologists.

The American Psychological Association (APA) has a division of military psychology. This division encourages research and the application of psychological research to military problems. It is well respected and the research attracts a lot of funding, so what do they do? Up until the 1960s, military psychology was mainly concerned with the same issues that would concern any major employer of people:

- selection of appropriate staff
- matching people (soldiers) to machines
- training (military) specialists
- staff welfare.

An article in the *American Psychologist* by Windle and Vallance (1964) reflected the change that began to take place in military psychology during the 1960s. It suggested that psychology was turning its attention to paramilitary issues: for example, studies to investigate the political motivations of guerrilla fighters, the human factors in underground organisations, and so on. Some of the other issues that this new type of psychology investigated were:

- the effects of captivity
- interrogation techniques
- brainwashing.

Today military psychologists look at a range of issues including the psychology of military organisation, the psychology of military life and the psychology of combat. To be truthful, much of the research is classified as secret so we don't have a complete picture of what is being studied. Before we develop too many conspiracy theories however, let's have a look at some classic pieces of military psychology that raise some ethical issues.

Sensory deprivation

One of the most controversial contributions of psychology was the development of sensory deprivation (SD) techniques. Donald Hebb was a leading figure in Canadian psychology and received substantial funding from the military to investigate this phenomenon. The question that he studied concerned the response people have to being removed from the common sensations of everyday life. What happens if you are in a place with no obvious changes in sight, sound or temperature and with nothing to do?

Volunteer students were kept in isolation in an air-conditioned room. They wore translucent goggles so that they could only see a blur of light. The only sound they heard was a constant buzzing noise and they had to wear long cuffs so that they couldn't touch anything. As an incentive they were offered $20 for every day they could stay in the room, and they each had a panic button which they could press to obtain instant release. They were provided with a comfortable bed and decent food.

To start with the volunteers tended to sleep, but soon they found that it became increasingly difficult to concentrate and they developed an acute desire for any kind of stimulation to break the monotony. Many started to experience startling visual and auditory hallucinations and after a while were unable to distinguish waking from sleeping. Despite the high pay for just lying on their backs, only a few lasted more than two days and the most anyone lasted was five days. When released they were given simple psychological tests that showed that their perceptions had become very disorientated with objects appearing blurred and fuzzy. More important from the investigators' point of view, while under the SD they were found to be much more susceptible to any type of propaganda.

There have been many more studies on this including immersing people in lukewarm water to further reduce the stimulation (Lilly

1956), or just leaving people alone in a silent room (Smith and Lewty 1959). In all the studies it does not take long for the participants to have severe psychological reactions including disordered thinking, loss of identification, panic, body-image distortions and violent nightmares (Zubek 1969).

A variation on the SD technique was used by the British Army in Northern Ireland in the early days of the Troubles. Shallice (1973) reported on 12 internees who were subjected to a horrifying interrogation technique. In the gaps between direct interrogation, the men were hooded in a black woven bag, subjected to very loud white noise and forced to stand against a wall with their hands above their heads. They were required to stand there for up to 16 hours and if they moved they were beaten. The internees were required to wear loose boiler suits, were sleep deprived and put on a restricted diet. This treatment had a devastating effect on the men who had major physical, cognitive, and emotional responses. The harrowing story is told in *The Guinea Pigs* (McGuffin 1974) and you can read it on the internet (www. irishresistancebooks.com/guineapigs/guineapigs.htm).

The military interest in the SD studies is twofold: first how to prepare their own troops for the rigours of captivity; second, how to encourage prisoners to talk. It is this second aim that raises the ethical issues. From an absolutist point of view, it is wrong to subject people to psychological torture, but what if that person has information which might save the lives of thousands? Would you still give them a cup of tea and a biscuit? Nothing is easy in this moral maze.

Just in case you notice the dates of the research and think this is all rather dated, then read your newspapers about Guantanamo Bay. After the recent war in Afghanistan the US forces detained several hundred people and defined them as non-combatants rather than prisoners of war. These people were then shipped to Guantanamo Bay in Cuba so that they would be outside US law. They were held in conditions of sensory deprivation (look at the pictures). The US military were hopeful of getting information about terrorist organisations from these prisoners.

Animals at war

Animals have been trained using behavioural techniques to become agents of human warfare. Most recently in the Iraq War (2003) seals were used to put handcuffs on enemy divers (SunSpot.net 2003; The Guardian 2003). In the past an ark-full of animals have been enlisted including cats, dogs, seagulls, dolphins and pigeons. Most famously B.F. Skinner showed that it was possible to use pigeons as a guidance system in a missile. To cut a long though interesting story short, Skinner (1960) showed that his pigeons could accurately pilot a missile to seek out ships, and could then discriminate between different types of ships so that they could fly past allied ships and dive onto enemy ships. The military got as far as modifying some of their missiles to accommodate the pigeons and their tracking apparatus. However, the pigeons were never brought into active service.

Many readers might be appalled at the callous disregard for the pigeons. If the project had been brought into operation, Skinner would have trained pigeons who would then unwittingly be the agents of their own destruction as they guided themselves and their missiles towards detonation on enemy ships. Ethics, however, must always be seen in the context of the times. During World War II (1939–45) it appeared to many people that it was right to go to war against Nazism, and that this war should be concluded as soon as possible to avoid defeat and further loss of life. Skinner writes: 'The ethical question of our right to convert a lower creature into an unwitting hero is a peace-time luxury.' You might still not accept this as a justification for the use of animals in warfare, but it does highlight that the issue of ethics is not a simple one and that people sometimes choose to act by criteria that conflict with their normal moral standards.

If we look back at the categories of ethical judgements first described in Chapter 1, then we might argue that the *consequences* of using animals in warfare (that is, reducing the number of human deaths and injuries) provide an adequate justification.

Psy-Ops (Psychological Operations)

Psychology has been used as a weapon of war. Most commonly it is used in the form of propaganda either to demoralise the enemy or to keep the home population on side. The example we are going to look at is of the US operations in Vietnam. This is not because the Americans are the only people to use these tactics, nor are they by any stretch of the imagination the worst, but they are the most reported and recorded army anywhere and so the information is readily available.

It is hard to say when the Vietnam War started. In 1945 Ho Chi Minh proclaimed the Democratic Republic of Vietnam and initiated the final struggle to get rid of the French colonial rulers from his country. Interestingly, he looked to the USA as a friend of this new republic and used the words of the US Declaration of Independence in his speech. The French were finally driven out ten years later, but not before the USA had started to become involved against the democratic aspirations of the Vietnamese people. This involvement was gradually increased and a military government that was favourable to the USA was established in the south of the country. For a ten-year period in the mid-1960s and 1970s the USA waged full-scale war against the Vietnamese people. To this day, it is not clear why they did it. The war ended in 1975 when the Americans were finally driven out of the country by the peasant army of the Vietnamese. At least 1,300,000 people were killed in the conflict[1] and many thousands more were maimed. Of the dead, 58,022 were Americans (less than 5 per cent), the rest were Vietnamese (Pilger 1989). It is one of the triumphs of western propaganda that this war is seen today as America's tragedy. Our view of this conflict is seen through the eyes of the Americans and we rarely hear the voice of the Vietnamese people telling us how a poorly armed, rural people managed to endure mass destruction and mass murder, and go on to defeat the greatest fighting force on the planet.[2]

One of the main strands of Psy-Ops were propaganda campaigns to change the opinions and the behaviour of the Vietnamese people. A review by Watson (1980) of the US propaganda campaigns during the Vietnam War suggests that great efforts were made to encourage defection by Vietnamese fighters. He quotes from military papers which estimate that during the month of March 1969 the American forces dropped 713,000,000 leaflets and distributed a further 3,000,000 by hand – all trying to encourage defection. During the same month 156,000 posters were distributed and 2000 hours of broadcasting were used for the same purpose. The military report does not estimate the effectiveness of this campaign but does note that the best way to encourage defection was through the stories of fighters who had already defected.

Watson (1980) suggests Psy-Op propaganda tactics commonly attempted to obtain a lot of cultural information so that they could better know how to influence the local people. He quotes military documents that show a social profile drawn up on a range of countries. These profiles included such information as:

- prestigious people
- common gifts used by people to get to know each other
- waste and disposal patterns
- attitudes to leaders
- the opinions of these leaders.

They also collected information on social and religious customs, including such items as what smells each culture found most offensive. The propaganda tactic was then to target particular attitudes, particular prominent people and particular customs and beliefs. One example of this approach concerned the grieving practices of the Vietnamese. It was the Vietnamese custom to remember deaths after 49 days and after 100 days as well as on anniversaries. Leaflets were dropped by the Americans on these dates after big battles in areas where people would have been likely to have lost relatives. The aim was to increase the misery of those days and further undermine the morale of the Vietnamese.

This example shows a remarkable cultural sensitivity. It makes use of detailed knowledge about customs and religious practices gathered by anthropologists and cross-cultural psychologists. It illustrates how being sensitive is not the same as being nice because this knowledge was used against the very people who were studied.

Ethical issues in military psychology

So what are the ethical issues about military psychology? We have raised the negatives in the examples given, but it is possible to argue a positive case for the use of psychology in the military. We might argue that the use of psychology can reduce injury or loss of life. Anything that speeds up a conflict will bring nearer the time of peace. We might also argue that some conflicts are morally justified and therefore it is appropriate to use psychology to advance the cause. It is also worth pointing out that much of the work of military psychologists is in the management of service personnel and their care and protection. Psychology has a lot to say about the response of combatants and civilians to warfare and can make some valuable contributions (Summerfield 2000).

Another ethical issue appears in a surprising way. In the work described above, the psychologists are attempting to show cultural sensitivity and become more aware of the customs and beliefs of diverse peoples. Gathering the information is fine and contributes to cultural understanding, but the ethical issue comes into play when the decision is made to use this information to terrorise people.

The easier ethical issue concerns the decision to take part or not. The more complicated issues arise after you have decided on that one. Psychologists who decide to take part in military activity still have to draw lines. It is also fair to say that those of us who decide not to take part still enjoy the benefits of living in a successful and militarily powerful society, so we can't just wash our hands of it and protest our innocence.

Progress exercise

List the reasons that you think make going to war justified and those that do not. For example, you might think that war is justified if you are being attacked.

Then try and list what psychology can be used for in warfare and consider when they might be justified. For example, psychology can be used to boost the morale of the home country and to demoralise the country we are at war with.

The conduct of psychologists

The behaviour of professional psychologists raises a number of ethical issues. They make contributions to the media, they have personal interactions with clients which are guided by a code of conduct and they develop theories and techniques that have a direct effect on the public.

Psychologists and the media

Psychologists have become increasingly involved with the media over the last 20 years[3] commonly offering advice on personal problems and comments on behaviour and events (Canter and Breakwell 1986). Newspaper advice columns, magazine self-improvement articles, psychology books, radio phone-in shows, talk show appearances, experts on the television news and consultants for films and television shows are among the many opportunities for psychologists to be in the media (Bouhoutsos *et al*. 1986).

Raviv *et al*. (1989) noted that the window of opportunity opened for psychomedia with the revision to the American Psychiatric Association Code of Ethics in 1981 permitting 'personal advice' but not 'therapy' on the air. The ambiguity between personal advice and therapy led to and continues to create a lot of controversy, but it also gave the green light to a new genre of media psychology.

Because psychologists are looked upon as experts in the field of human relations, they are also often interviewed by journalists to shed light on a particular issue, incident, or area of interest (Frank 1983). This can become a problem as information is often presented in a superficial way in the media due to time demand or space limitations, and thus a psychologist's statements may be misinterpreted or presented inaccurately. We need to develop a new ethical code to deal with these interactions. Box 6.1 shows some suggestions offered by Keith-Spiegel and Koocher (1985).

It is fair to say that many psychologists are very careful about their dealings with the media but this is a text about ethical issues so we will look at some examples of psychologist's work that raise concerns.

Inside the mind of Paul Gascoigne

On 10 July 2003, Channel 4 showed a film entitled 'Inside the Mind of Paul Gascoigne'. Gascoigne is a professional footballer (oh you must have heard of him) of exceptional talent who has attracted massive media attention for most of his adult life. This programme set out to show that he is in some mental distress and to provide as many labels as possible for that distress. As *The Guardian* wrote the next day 'Where would TV be without experts?' The programme used experts including psychologist Professor Kevin Gournay to suggest that Gascoigne is suffering from three varieties of mental disorder: attention deficit disorder, obsessive-compulsive disorder and Tourette's syndrome. The diagnosis was reached without a personal examination of Gascoigne, but as *The Guardian*'s television reviewer wrote, 'Professor Kevin Gournay seemed pretty convinced'. Once Gournay had provided the academic gloss to this programme, Gascoigne's friends and colleagues queued up to report how 'mad' he is. Subsequent press reports now

---

Box 6.1   Suggestions for psychologists dealing with the media (Keith-Spiegel and Koocher 1985)

1. Find out the purpose of the story, if it sounds exploitive, consider waiting for another opportunity to make your material public.

2. Give the reporter a written statement, if possible, to reduce the chance of misquotes.

3. Invite the reporter to call you back if questions arise, or for an editorial review.

4. Refuse comment on an area where you have insufficient knowledge and, if possible, make a referral to an informed source.

5. Call back if you believe you made an error.

6. Qualify all salient or dramatic remarks and avoid making offhanded comments.

7. Do not speak for the profession as a whole.

8. Admit when you do not have an answer, rather than formulating an ill-informed one.

9. If the topic is controversial, suggest that the reporter contact other colleagues as well.

10. Offer only possibilities when asked to comment on situations on which no solid data exists (e.g. a hostage situation).

11. Psychological evaluations about newsworthy individuals should be avoided and confidentiality should be observed at all times.

12. If you are dissatisfied about the final product, let the reporter know in a constructive way.

---

commonly describe Gascoigne with the diagnostic labels used in the programme. On the Channel 4 website (www.channel4.com/health/microsites/P/paul_gascoigne/index.html) it says:

> According to psychologists, Paul's manic energy, short attention span and childish, inappropriate behaviour are all symptoms of a mental condition known as Attention Deficit Disorder (ADD). Paul also appears to suffer from Obsessive Compulsive Disorder (OCD), an illness where overwhelming anxiety is relieved by repetitive behaviour, such as obsessive tidying or over-exercising.

Paul admits to such obsessive behaviours, but puts them down to stress; they were his way of handling a situation that he wasn't happy with. Furthermore, his well-documented twitches, grimaces and outbursts are classic symptoms of a neurological disorder that often accompanies OCD – Tourette Syndrome.

Let's unpick the ethics of this. If Gascoigne were a patient of Gournay, then the therapist would not be at liberty to discuss him for reasons of confidentiality. Gournay can only discuss him because he doesn't know him. But what are the professional ethics of commenting on someone you have never met and publicly attaching damaging psychiatric labels to them? Gascoigne disputes this diagnosis but his point of view is not given the same weight as that of the absent expert. Furthermore, if Gascoigne does indeed have some serious mental health problems, then how is his welfare helped by Gournay's contribution? Has he not further added to the distress of the man and thereby amplified whatever problems he had? Is there not an alternative explanation for Gascoigne's behaviour in his victimisation by the media for many years? Gournay might well have commented on the psychological pressure of not even being able to have a pizza without someone taking a photograph of him, though that might not have fitted the agenda of the programme and he wouldn't have got his generous cheque. Professor Gournay is a very wise man, and very wise men make a point of saying what people want to hear.

The Big Brother psychologists

The *Big Brother* programmes are a (western) worldwide phenomena. A group of young people are put in a house and observed 24 hours a day. They are given strict rules of behaviour so they cannot challenge the nature of the show or define their own lives. They are effectively human goldfish. One of the regular features is for psychologists to comment on their behaviour and their relationships. Here is an example of these comments as reported on the *Big Brother* website (bigbrother. digitalspy.co.uk/article/ds419.html):

Psychologist Geoffrey Beattie has been studying the house-mates' different reactions to newcomer Claire. His attention, in these early stages in particular, is focused on Mel. From the first introductions, the psychology team noticed behavioural traits that separated Mel from the rest of the group. 'Mel's posture was very closed towards Claire,' said Beattie. 'The others as a group were very open.'

Even Mel's smile came under scrutiny. 'It was a strange smile that abruptly changed to a neutral expression, hinting that it was never a genuine smile at all. Claire is a threat to Mel. So far, Mel has had most of the boys running after her. What we can expect to see now is Mel being more pro-active with her flirting. She has competition and will have to put in more effort.

What are the ethical issues in this you may ask? Isn't it just harmless entertainment? As ever, it depends on your view of what is happening. We would argue that (a) it misrepresents psychology and (b) is potentially damaging to the contestants. On the first point, we have to be clear that psychologists *cannot* read minds, *cannot* read intentions, *cannot* read body language, *cannot* read palms and *cannot* see into the future. They cannot tell everything about you from looking at your body language and, while we're at it, they cannot read tea leaves or handwriting. Beattie's comments can be seen as harmless nonsense but many viewers might believe there is some academic weight behind them. The second point follows on from the first, in that viewers put more weight on the words of professionals such as psychologists than is appropriate. They may well build up an impression of the contestants that is wholly wrong, and this impression might well persist even after they have left the house.

The upside of psychology on the media is that it can bring psychological ideas to the general public. It can inform and educate, but it can also trivialise and obfuscate.

Psychologists and therapy

One of the most prominent areas of professional psychology is to provide support to people with mental or behavioural disorders. This contact with distressed and vulnerable people provides psychologists with great opportunities to contribute positively to our society but also raises some socially sensitive ethical issues.

Manufacturing victims

Professional workers need clients or they are out of a job. Doctors need patients, the police need criminals, soldiers need conflict and psychologists need the business. Mental distress is big business and psychologists have a part to play in that business. One part is to provide support and help to people who are in distress, but not everyone believes it stops there. Tana Dineen (1999) is a critic of the therapy industry (as she calls it) and, according to her, most psychologists do more harm than good and are actively engaged in the business of turning as many of us as possible into 'victims' prepared to pay for therapy.

Although much of her argument focuses on entrepreneurial psychology in North America, what she has to say is relevant to any society in which faith is placed in counsellors, therapists, trauma-tologists, and anyone else who happens to thinks they can explain all our current ills, from minor anxieties to crime and economic failure, in pseudo-psychological terms. What she objects to, in short, is quackery. In her book *Manufacturing Victims: What the Psychology Industry Is Doing to People* she describes many examples of it.

In some ways, of course, psychology is a soft target. The misuse of recovered memory therapy, where patients allegedly recover buried memories of sexual or satanic abuse (often with dramatic legal conse-quences), is easy to criticise. Absurdities like 'llama therapy' (where llamas are used to teach young offenders to feel empathy) and therapists offering treatment for people feeling 'enslaved by email' are even easier to deride. Dineen, however, isn't simply concerned about things that are obviously scandalous or absurd. She's concerned about the whole scientific foundation of the discipline. A large part of her book focuses on examples of fraudulent research and on the failure of psychologists to prove that their various therapies benefit anyone other than themselves.

Diagnostic and Statistical Manual of Mental Disorders (DSM)

One of the significant contributions of psychologists and psychiatrists to the treatment of mental disorders in the United States is the *Diagnostic and Statistical Manual of Mental Disorders* (DSM). The current version runs to 900 pages and describes more than 300 mental disorders. The DSM is used to classify mental disorders and give them a diagnosis. The DSM is an American invention though it is becoming increasingly used in the UK. The widely used international alternative is the World Health Organisation categories of illness, the *International Statistical Classification of Diseases and Related Health Problems* (ICD; see www.who.int/whosis/icd10/).

The DSM structures the way we think about life, behaviour and experience and defines many sorts of behaviour as mental disorders, some of which do not seem to deserve the label of mental disorder. For example, it has a disorder called Oppositional Defiant Disorder, something you or I might well call 'being awkward', and another disorder called Conduct Disorder which might be called 'naughtiness' by someone else.

The danger of the DSM is that it can turn everyday behaviour into pathological categories, thereby creating work for psychologists among others, and assigning negative labels to ordinary people. In case you think we are exaggerating the problem, you might consider an article in a prestigious journal that reports that one-third of us have 'excessive anxiety' when asked to speak to large audiences and may be suffering from a mental disorder (Stein *et al.* 1996). It seems entirely reasonable, to the authors, to be very anxious about speaking in public, especially to a big audience. It is difficult to see this anxiety as a sign of mental disorder.

The DSM raises ethical issues because of the behaviours it decides to classify as a disorder and because of the uses to which it is put. With regard to the first point there have been long and bitter debates over the years about how to classify homosexual behaviour and how to classify the behaviour of the women in abusive relationships. The way you classify these behaviours will affect how people are seen and dealt with, so it is not just a theoretical exercise. With regard to the uses of the DSM, it must be said that a diagnosis can be worth a lot of money. It can be worth money to the patient because if you want to sue an employer for causing your illness you have to have a diagnosis. It can also be worth a lot of money to the pharmaceutical industry because for every diagnosis there is a medication you can use. You might not be surprised to read that some of the main funders of DSM development are the pharmaceutical companies. The world thinks it is going mad because the drug companies tell it so, and psychologists collude in this nonsense because it is good for our business as well.[4]

The ethical issues that inevitably arise concern the care and welfare of the clients. Is their welfare being put in front of the commercial interests of the pharmaceutical companies, or is the reverse true? And are their interests best served with a label for their relatively common behaviour?

Post Traumatic Stress Disorder (PTSD)

The diagnosis of Post Traumatic Stress Disorder (PTSD) illustrates the problems of diagnosing socially sensitive problems. PTSD was first included in the DSM in 1980 as a response to demands from US veterans of the War in Vietnam to acknowledge the distressing symptoms that many of them experienced. Since then the diagnosis has been through many revisions in the DSM so that it is almost unrecognisable today. The original version stated that the events that triggered the response must be so unusual that they were 'outside the range of normal human experience.' This neatly fitted the extreme conditions of warfare and captivity. This phrase was deleted from later versions of the DSM and allowed all manner of experiences to be included. This change has dramatically expanded the use of the diagnosis of PTSD and hence the demand for treatment, medication and litigation. One phrase can create a multi-million pound market.

The problem with broad criteria for diagnosis is that it encourages over-diagnosis to the point where everyday experiences start being seen as requiring treatment. One of the main diagnostic measures for PTSD is the Impact of Events Scale. It is possible to get high (and pathological) measures on this scale for events such as the death of Diana Princess of Wales (Shevlin *et al*. 1997) and the relegation of your football team from the English Premier League (Banyard and Shevlin 2000). It is difficult to argue that if your team is relegated from the Premier League then you are in danger of experiencing PTSD. It might well be distressing, but it does not compare with the effects of, for example, being in an abusive prisoner of war camp.

Perhaps the most significant problem for the diagnosis of PTSD is its use with victims of violent crimes such as rape, domestic violence and sexual abuse. Kirk and Kutchins (2002) ask whether health professionals need to make a diagnosis in order to understand that victims need all the help they can get. They argue that it is a disservice to victims to give them a diagnosis because they are suffering from the after-effects of a traumatic event. Is it appropriate to attach a psychiatric label to someone who is dealing with a traumatic event? Are we not just further victimising them?

Happiness

On a lighter note, Bentall (1992) parodied the DSM by proposing that happiness be classified as a mental disorder and renamed 'major affective disorder: pleasant type'. He suggested that a review of the relevant literature showed that happiness is statistically abnormal. It consists of a discrete cluster of symptoms, is associated with a range of cognitive abnormalities and probably reflects the abnormal functioning of the nervous system. The parody highlights the ethical issues that arise from diagnosing more and more of our behaviour as pathological. The diagnosis of everyday behaviour as being disordered leads to a growing dependency on the psychology industry and a decreased confidence of ordinary people in their ability to live their lives competently.

Relationships with clients

The issue of sexual involvement between therapist and patients is an obvious area of concern. It is clearly difficult to get accurate data on this topic as people are unlikely to willingly disclose their behaviour. Given that, the survey data is quite remarkable. A recent meta-analysis of surveys on this issue by Pope (2001) found that 7 per cent of male therapists and 1.5 per cent of female therapists admitted to sexual intimacies with their clients (Table 6.1).

This behaviour would appear to be unethical because of the trust put in the therapist by the patient. It does not seem likely that therapists can remove themselves totally from the powerful role they have when they take on another role with the patient. So it would appear to be unethical, but is it harmful? Pope and Vetter (1991) published a study of 958 patients who had been sexually involved with a therapist. The findings suggest that about 90 per cent of patients are harmed by sex with a therapist, though this drops slightly to 80 per cent when the sexual involvement begins only after termination of therapy. About 11 per cent required hospitalisation, 14 per cent attempted suicide and 1 per cent committed suicide. About 10 per cent had experienced rape prior to sexual involvement with the therapist, and about a third had

Table 6.1 *Studies on the sexual relations between therapist and clients (Pope 2001)*

Study	Publication date	Discipline	Sample size	Return rate %	Male therapists reporting sex with clients %	Female therapists reporting sex with clients %
Holroyd and Brodsky	1977	Psychologists	1000	70.0	12.1	2.6
Pope, Levenson and Schover	1979	Psychologists	1000	48.0	12.0	3.0
Pope, Keith-Spiegel and Tabachnick	1986	Psychologists	1000	58.5	9.4	2.5
Gartrell, Herman, Olarte, Feldstein and Localio	1986	Psychiatrists	5574	26.0	7.1	3.1
Pope, Tabachnick and Keith-Spiegel	1987	Psychologists	1000	46.0	3.6	0.4
Akamatsu	1988	Psychologists	1000	39.5	3.5	2.3
Borys and Pope	1989	Psychiatrists, psychologists and social workers	4800	56.5	0.9	0.2
Bernsen, Tabachnick and Pope	1994	Social workers	1000	45.3	3.6	0.5

experienced incest or other child sex abuse. About 5 per cent of these patients were minors at the time of the sexual involvement with the therapist. Of those harmed, only 17 per cent recovered fully.

You might argue that it's a fact of life that when people spend time together they sometimes become attracted to each other and sometimes have occasional intimacies, but there is a growing sense that many of these relationships are ethically questionable: the doctor with the patient, the teacher with the student, the boss with the employee, the police officer with the criminal. All these relationships lead to conflicts of interest and might well harm the very people we are trying to help.

This all seems a sorry state of affairs when you read the above: psychologists creating victims, categorising them, treating them inappropriately and then having sex with them. We hasten to add that we are not suggesting that most or even much of psychological practice is unsound or damaging. We chose to look at this information in order to wrestle with the complex ethical dilemmas faced by professional people when they carry out their work. In theory we can all be the most ethical person in the world, but in everyday life it is not so easy.

Speaking out

Can we avoid ethical dilemmas by avoiding all sensitive issues and keeping quiet? We would argue that psychologists have an ethical and moral responsibility to speak out on some important issues. The ethical problems are related to having to choose when to speak out and having to choose what to say as a psychologist. If we consider military actions, for example, then Britain has been involved in three major conflicts in the last five years, in Kosovo, in Afghanistan and in Iraq. Psychological research has contributed a lot to our understanding about the behaviour of armies in warfare, the experience of civilians in warfare and the long-term effects of warfare on military personnel and civilians. Considering that you often can't switch on the TV without hearing from a psychologist, it is remarkable how silent the profession has been about these military actions.

There has been the occasional article in the professional journals (for example, Sloboda and Coleman 2000), but little to no comment in the mainstream media. Sloboda (2001) suggests that one of the reasons psychologists give for their silence is the code of conduct which says that they should not comment outside their area of specialism and competence. As discussed about the *Big Brother* psychologists and the TV diagnosticians, psychologists are often happy to stretch this guideline without comment from the profession. Sloboda questions how much competence we need to point out the negative effects of warfare. If we are not competent then don't we have a responsibility to find out about these things. If psychology is the study of mind and behaviour then surely the professional bodies such as the British Psychological Society (BPS) should have something to say about the mind and behaviour of military action.

A strange exception to the silence of psychologists over the effects of war and terrorism was the reaction to the destruction of the Twin Towers in New York on 11th September 2001. Bear in mind that the USA has the most psychologists in the world and is the wealthiest country in the world. Then consider that the first official response of the BPS was to offer help and support on behalf of British psychologists to psychologists working in New York with the bereaved and the traumatised. As Sloboda (2001) remarks, is there any city on the planet with more psychologists than New York? The offer appears all the more strange given that no equivalent offer appears to have been to made to the citizens of Yugoslavia, Afghanistan or Iraq who endured months or even years of bombing by western forces. If you are uncomfortable with the military side of that dilemma, then look for the offers of psychological support to scenes of natural disasters or famine in the developing world.

Summary

The chapter appears to be a stinging critique of psychology, and we have raised some disturbing examples of unethical practice. By way of balance it is important to note that if we applied the same criteria to nearly any other profession we would find similar dilemmas. For example, in the medical profession there are many dubious relationships between practitioners and pharmaceutical companies, and we don't even know where to start with lawyers or journalists because we'd fill the rest of the book.

Socially sensitive issues create ethical dilemmas: for the profession, to speak out or to remain silent, to consider the individual or the wider community; for researchers, to ensure that people do not disclose more than they wished, to respect the clients; for individual psychologists, speaking out, selecting their research topics, etc. It is easy to take the high moral ground and pick holes in everyone else. We hope we have not done this but have provided some reasoned debate on the dilemmas that face psychologists. Where you choose to stand on these dilemmas is up to you.

Further reading

Kutchins, H. and Kirk, S. (1997) *Making Us Crazy*, Constable: London (a readable critique of how the pharmaceutical industry and psychologists create the categories of mental ill health].

Websites

The Channel 4 website on the programme 'Inside the Mind of Paul Gascoigne' <www.channel4.com/health/microsites/P/paul_gascoigne/index.html>

The Big Brother website (also at Channel 4) where you can type 'psychologist' into the search and get a range of psychobabble responses <http://bigbrother.channel4.com/bigbrother/>

An article on the use of animals in warfare <www.sunspot.net/news/nationworld/iraq/bal-te.dolphins26mar26,0,1891645.story?coll= bal-home-headlines>

World Health Organisation site for the ICD <www.who.int/whosis/icd10/>

7

Psychological research with non-human animals

In this book we have been concerned with ethical issues and guidelines for human participants involved in psychological research. This chapter considers the use of non-human animals[1] in psychological research. There are two questions to ask:

1. To what extent is research with animals *valuable*?
2. To what extent is it *acceptable* or ethical?

In other words, in this chapter we are not just concerned with ethics but also with the questions of whether such research is useful or necessary. One thing to bear in mind as you read this chapter is that we are concerned with *psychological research*. The use of animals in medical research may be easier to justify than their use in psychological research; whereas their use in, for example, cosmetic research may be less easy to justify. We will *focus* on psychological research.

Another thing to bear in mind is *emotion*. It is easy to become emotional about the maltreatment of cute and cuddly puppies but to feel less strongly about slippery slimy fish. Your task is to dispassionately weigh the evidence and arguments rather than being blinded by your emotions and prejudices – or to at least acknowledge your prejudices.

A third consideration is *context*. Context is everything. What might appear unethical here and now might seem perfectly acceptable in a different environment. You might be a vegetarian with a belief that it is morally wrong (unethical) to eat meat, but if you had the choice of eating meat or dying of starvation then you would probably see your survival as more important than your belief. In the previous chapter we noted the use of animals in warfare and the work of animal psychologists in modern warfare. The belief that affects your final judgement of the ethics of this work is how necessary you believe the war is. If you were fighting for your survival then you might well think it is acceptable to use animals as agents of war, but if you saw the conflict as a fight over oil supplies, for example, then you would probably see the use of animals as unacceptable. The same points can be applied to your belief in psychological research. The point here is that the judgement of the ethics of using animals is not clear cut nor can it ever be so. A summary of the attitudes of psychology students to animal testing is shown in Box 7.1.

The chapter starts with a review of the use of animals in psychological research just to give you a platform for thinking about this kind of research. Next we review constraints currently in place that govern the use of animals. Finally we turn to the question of usefulness (whether the research is valuable) and ethics (whether the research is acceptable).

Examples of research with non-human animals

The mention of animal research may conjure up in your mind a picture of a dog pinned down to a dissection table. Cast such images from your mind. We are concerned with psychological research and very little psychological research involves operating theatres. The sort of issues that will concern us are whether an animal's behaviour or physiology is affected by the research procedures in such a way that the animal's subsequent life is altered. We are also concerned with the care of

Box 7.1 Support for animal research in psychology

This graph shows the margin of support American psychology students expressed for various types of research. Respondents were given an empty table with four columns labelled Primates, Dogs, Rats, Pigeons, and three rows labelled:

- Observational studies in naturalistic settings.
- Research involving caging or confinement, but no physical pain or death.
- Research involving physical pain or death.

They were told to assume that the research was 'institutionally approved and deemed of scientific merit' and asked to indicate whether each type of research was usually justified or unjustified. The margin of support equals the percentage of respondents saying it was justified minus the percentage of respondents saying it was unjustified (Plous 1996).

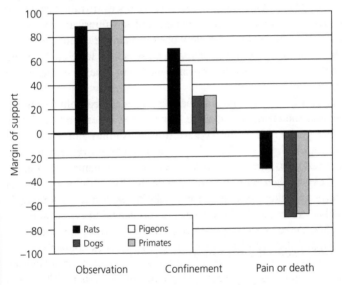

You can see from the graph that context was everything – research with non-human animals was acceptable in observational research, slightly less acceptable when confinement was involved and unacceptable if pain or death were involved.

animals before, during and after being participants in research; it isn't just the procedures performed by a psychologist but the general care of the research participant.

This is not to suggest psychological research is relatively harmless. Some research has involved invasive procedures on animal participants and we will consider that first.

Harlow's monkeys

A very well known series of experiments was led by Harry Harlow in the 1950s. His early research on learning with rhesus monkeys led him to breed his own monkeys in captivity in order to improve their survival rates. The monkeys were brought up in separate cages to reduce the chances of infection and they developed a number of unusual and damaging behaviours that are not commonly observed in animals. The striking thing to the observers was that the behaviours such as repetitive movements, rocking and self-injury are commonly seen in disturbed humans. Harlow observed that when he released his isolated monkeys from their individual cages they were unable to get on with other monkeys and appeared unable to develop normal social relationships or even mate.

The disturbed and damaging behaviour developed from the attempt to reduce the chances of disease and was not anticipated by Harlow (1959). As such it would be hard to criticise him and his research team for unethical conduct. There is a problem, however, with what happened next. Having found that isolation had a damaging effect on monkeys he then set out to investigate this by deliberately creating disturbed monkeys through further isolation experiments. Among the popularly recorded findings are that his orphan monkeys became very attached to the cloth nappies used to line their cage. This led him to investigate the hypothesis that young animals seek contact comfort. He did this through a series of experiments involving monkeys and two wire 'mothers' – one covered in cloth and the other with no cloth but a feeding bottle. The monkeys showed a surprising preference for the cloth mothers, demonstrating the importance of contact comfort in attachment. Harlow (1959) tested different variations such as blasting the young monkeys with air to test the effects of abusive mothering. It appeared that the monkeys formed an even stronger attachment to 'abusive mothers'.

The work is sometimes justified as providing a valuable insight into the development of attachment and social behaviour. At the time of the research there was a dominant belief that attachment was related to physical rather than emotional care. It was the fashion in parts of American society for adults to be remote from children and not very affectionate. The theoretical work of John Bowlby and others such as Robert Hinde challenged such views. Harlow's research was used as empirical support for these theories. It is arguable as to how important this research evidence was. It may be that it was totally unnecessary (there was also research with human infants) or it may actually have been vital in convincing people about the importance of emotional care in hospitals, children's homes and childcare generally.

Operant training

B.F. Skinner conducted a large number of laboratory experiments to demonstrate the principles and application of operant conditioning. For example, a rat would be placed in a box with a lever. If the lever was pressed a pellet of food was delivered. This acted as a reinforcer and the rat acquired a new behaviour. This all sounds quite jolly and the rat appears to be having the life of Riley sitting around all day in a cosy box just pressing levers for food. Sadly, it was not all joy for the rats even when it appeared so.

The work of Olds and Milner (1954) is an illustration of this. They were interested in what makes something pleasurable. We find things like food or drink or sex pleasurable, but why? What is pleasure? They investigated this using rats in a Skinner Box. Instead of getting food when they pressed the lever the rats received a brief electric shock to the brain through a small wire implanted in their heads. You would imagine that an electrical current to the brain would be very unpleasant, in which case the rat would press the lever only once or twice before scuttling off to the other side of the cage as far away from the lever as possible. This was not, however, the outcome of the study.

The results show that the rats continued to press the lever when the wire was in the septal area of their brains. In other words they chose to give themselves electrical stimulation when given the opportunity. They spent, on average, 85 per cent of their time regularly pressing the lever to obtain the stimulation. One rat stimulated itself with lever presses over 7500 times in 12 hours at an average of 742 responses an hour, or more than once every 5 seconds. We have to conclude that the lever pressing, and hence the stimulation, was very reinforcing. Before you start thinking to yourself that you'd like to be connected up to something that seems so much fun, it is worth pointing out that the rats paid a price for this fun. Olds and Milner report that 'after testing the animal was sacrificed' (p. 419), and its brain was examined to find the exact location of the electrode.

The ethical judgement centres around whether you think this work provides valuable insights that will have tangible benefits. If you think the work of the behaviourists has scientific and social merit then the use of animals is justifiable and possibly ethical, but if you do not accept the scientific merit of the work then the ethical justification becomes harder to make.

It is also worth noting that when we talk about laboratory rats we are not referring to the friendly rat at the bottom of your garden or in your cellar. This wild rat is a lively little chap capable of spectacularly quick learning as well as transporting some of the most deadly diseases the world has ever known (plague, botulism, etc.). The laboratory rat is an altogether different animal. They have been selectively bred over many generations for their docility and ability to deal with the laboratory environment. They would not survive for long if they were released in the gardens and cellars of Britain. This adds a further question mark over the work because we are looking at behaviour of a manufactured species in a manufactured environment and trying to apply it to real-life problems.

Sensory deprivation

One technique used to investigate development is to deprive an animal (or person) of part of its normal experience and see what the long-term consequences are. It is argued that this technique allows us to investigate the relative effects of genetics and learning in any behaviour. The work of Harlow (1959) can be seen as a deprivation design in that the animals were deprived of normal social contact during the first months of life. This technique has been extensively used in the study of perception.

Some of the earliest studies of this type investigated what happens to an animal if it is brought up without any visual stimulation, in other words kept in the dark. The point of these studies was to find out whether the animals had to learn to see from scratch when they finally were brought into the light or whether they would have some innate visual abilities which were unaffected by experience. Studies by Riesen (1956), for example, found that cats, chimpanzees and other animals did not develop their full visual abilities while being raised in total darkness. In fact the experience left them unable ever to see properly in their lives. Light deprivation seems to have severe effects on the perceptual system, and this occurs even if the deprivation is only in one eye. Hubel *et al.* (1977) surgically closed one eye of two-week-old monkeys and found their visual systems subsequently did not develop normally.

A refinement on the sensory deprivation technique is to provide restricted stimulation rather than no stimulation. A particularly famous study was conducted on kittens in restricted environments (Blakemore and Cooper 1970). In one of these studies the kittens only had early experience of either vertical or horizontal lines rather than a full visual world. When tested after five months of living in this restricted environment they were able to get around normally but were virtually blind to lines which were perpendicular to those they had been exposed to in their restricted environment (i.e. the kittens raised with vertical lines often tripped over strings stretched between two chairs – a horizontal line).

You might well ask why a zoo-full of animals and birds has been blinded and deafened, but the scientist might argue that there has been some benefit in our knowledge of sensory processes and therefore our treatment of people with sensory deficits (as we will see later). Other work by Hubel and Wiesel (1962) discovered the areas of the brain responsible for perceiving the orientation of lines, and this work brought them a Nobel Prize. It is easy to be critical of all animal research, but before you dismiss it out of hand it is important to weigh up the possible benefits of some studies.

Field studies

We should also consider research conducted in more natural environments. For example, Gardner and Gardner (1969) raised a chimpanzee called Washoe in their own home and taught her to use sign language, achieving a reasonable degree of success. The reason for training the chimpanzee in a home environment was so that the animal could acquire language as children do – as part of everyday life. This means that the chimpanzees were enculturated into human society and removed from their natural lifestyle and culture. When the investigation was over the researchers had a duty to provide lifelong care for this primate (which they did, see websites at the end of this chapter). However, not all primates used in psychological research have been so lucky, though there are a growing number of facilities that provide care for animals once research projects are finished.

We might consider another well-known field study also concerned with animal communication. Seyfarth and Cheney (1980) demonstrated how vervet monkeys use different alarm calls. They did this by recording the monkeys' calls in response to different predators and playing these back to other monkeys to demonstrate that different calls had specific meanings. The effect may be that monkeys hearing such calls in the absence of any predator may learn not to respond. This could endanger their lives in the future should they fail to respond to alarm calls involving real predators.

Naturalistic observations

It is important to remember that there are a number of studies conducted on animal behaviour which are purely observational and involve no interference with the animals being studied: for example, Dian Fossey's work observing gorillas in their natural habitat to reach a greater understanding of their social relationships, made famous through the film *Gorillas in the Mist*.

However, psychological research does tend to be more of the investigational variety, where some variables have been manipulated to observe the effects on behaviour and such manipulations raise ethical concerns.

Constraints on animal research

Ironically, the first case of child abuse ever brought to court relied on legislation for the protection of animals. In the 1870s a 9-year-old child, Mary Ellen Wilson, had been beaten, cut and burned by her foster mother for more than seven years. A concerned social worker made appeals to police, the church and the courts, but with no success. As a last resort she turned to the American Society for the Prevention of Cruelty to Animals. They brought Mary Ellen's case to court arguing that she was a member of the animal kingdom and therefore deserved the same protection (Shelman and Lazoritz 1999). At the time there were laws protecting animals but no laws protecting children. So there is a longer history of protection of animals than children.

Animal research in the UK is governed by the Animals Act (Scientific Procedures) Act 1986. Psychological research in the UK is guided by the BPS Code of Conduct. A summary of both these documents is given in Boxes 7.2 and 7.3.

Box 7.2 The Animals (Scientific Procedures) Act 1986 – main points

1. **The law**. Failure to comply with the law will lead to prosecution and possible custodial sentences. Any procedure that causes pain or distress to animals is illegal unless the researcher holds a Home Office licence. This is only given if there are no alternatives available and suffering is minimised.

2. **Ethical considerations**. Investigators must consider whether the knowledge to be gained from any investigation justifies harm or distress to animal participants. Alternatives should be considered where possible.

3. **Species**. When selecting animal participants researchers might consider the fact that some species may be less likely to suffer than others. It is important to be aware of the natural history of any animal participants and their special needs, and avoid the use of endangered species.

4. **Number of animals**. The number of animals required in any investigation can be reduced through the use of careful design.

5. **Caging and social environment**. The environment used to house research animals should take into account their natural social behaviours, for example, social animals should not be kept in isolation.

6. **Motivation**. When designing experiments that involve rewards or deprivation the experimenter should consider an animal's normal eating and drinking habits and metabolic requirements.

Box 7.3 BPS Code of Conduct for use of non-human animals in research

The British Psychological Society has produced a code of conduct for psychologists conducting research with non-human animals. Such codes of conduct are not laws but any psychologists found to have contravened the code may be struck off the professional register. The main points of the BPS code in relation to research with non-human animals are:

- *Legislation*. Psychologists must conform to current legislation.
- *Choice of species*. Should be suited to research purpose and psychologist should be aware of animal's previous experience.
- *Number of animals*. The smallest number should be used.
- *Procedures*. Any procedure that may cause pain should be carefully evaluated and alternatives considered. Regulation of food intake (e.g. for conditioning experiments) may be considered to be harmful and researchers should consider an animal's normal food intake and metabolic requirements. Investigators studying animals in the field should minimise interference.

Progress exercise

Identify three key points that appear both in the Animals Act and BPS Code of Conduct related to the constraints on the use of animals in psychological research.

Summarising the constraints

The main concerns, in relation to psychological research using animals are:

1. *Preventing harm*. Clearly harm should be avoided as far as possible. The cost-benefit principle operates in the same way as it does for

research with human participants (as discussed on pages 34–6). Suffering may be justified by the importance of the research.

2. *Limiting numbers.* The acceptability of animal research may be higher if fewer animals are used.

3. *Seeking alternatives.* Animal research is also made more acceptable if it is clear that, where possible, alternatives are used, such as computer simulations or tissue cultures.

4. *Attention to individual needs.* If animals are used then it is clearly important that researchers are familiar with the needs of the particular species. For example, some animals may find certain stimuli distressing where others don't. Some animals may cope well without food for several days but this would not be true for other species.

5. *The care of animals.* Researchers have a duty of care to their animal participants; i.e. adequate housing during and sometimes after research has taken place.

You should note that many of these points apply equally to invasive procedures and non-invasive procedures (i.e. involving no harm).

Guiding principles

A report by the House of Lords (2002) identifies the importance of the three Rs as guiding principles in the design of animal research. The three Rs were first proposed by Russell and Birch (1959). Where possible researchers should:

- *Refine* the experimental procedures to minimise suffering
- *Reduce* the number of animals used to the minimum required to support sound risk assessments to protect humans, animals and the environment
- *Replace* the use of animals, for example, by in vitro methods.

Exempted species

Many countries now ban research with certain animals such as all great apes, including chimpanzees, bonobos, gorillas, orangutans, and some gibbons. Such animals are regarded as being sufficiently close to humans as to ignore their rights (a topic we will return to later).

Included in the list of countries operating such a ban is Great Britain, Japan, New Zealand, Sweden, the Netherlands.

Commentary

Clearly animal research is carefully regulated both by the law and by professional codes of conduct. However, it has been argued that in a way so-called 'animal' laws legitimise abuse (Dunayer 2002). Dunayer argues that such laws simply set standards for the imprisonment, enslavement, hurting and killing of animals. Such laws are similar to the laws that codified norms of black enslavement in the USA. Making it legal doesn't make it right. It can be argued that 'animal' laws should be abolished. They could be replaced with laws that prohibit humans from violating non-human rights. The same laws that protect humans would then protect non-humans, extending to them all applicable rights currently reserved for humans.

This sounds very worthy but there is a problem with the idea of animal rights (see Chapter 1). If we extend human rights to cover animals as well, then we would have to grant them freedom from oppression, a right to paid holiday, a right to nationality and freedom of association (UN Declaration of Human Rights, see Box 1.4).[2] I don't know about you, but the local cat community is not allowed the right of free association in my garden.

Another critical point concerns the problem with guidelines in general. Such guidelines (codes of conduct) remove any need for a researcher to think about what they are doing in terms of right and wrong. Instead a researcher may feel no ethical responsibility because it 'has been done for him'. Following the code is sufficient to ensure ethical behaviour. In a surprising way ethical guidelines can discourage ethical thinking and a sense of ethical responsibility.

Usefulness: the scientific arguments for using animals in research

To what extent is research with animals valuable? There are various ways to consider this question: First, to be considered is the behaviourist argument that animal behaviour is structured by the same principles which structure human behaviour and therefore one can find out about human behaviour by using animals. Second to be considered is the value of physiological research using animals. Many animals have similar physiological systems to humans and therefore we can find out about human physiology by studying animal physiology. Third to be considered is the importance of studying animals simply to find out about animals.

Generalising from animal to human behaviour

Behaviourists use the theory of evolution to argue that since animals and humans share common ancestors they are composed of the same basic building blocks – behavioural as well as physiological. In humans these building blocks build up to more complex behaviours but the basic units are the same: stimulus–response units that explain conditioning. So, for example, by demonstrating learned helplessness in animals we can generalise to human behaviour and assume that the same principles apply.

For those who are not familiar with this research, Seligman and Maier (1967) placed dogs in a cage where they could not escape from electric shocks being given to their hindlegs. Later the same dogs were placed in a different cage where they could escape into a different compartment. In this new environment the dogs did not attempt to move to the safe part of the cage, whereas dogs who had not been exposed to the 'no escape' condition did escape. It was concluded that experience of a situation where escape from aversive stimuli is not possible leads to learning the behaviour of helplessness – a passive acceptable of an unpleasant situation. This principle was generalised to human behaviour as an explanation of depression.

Think of another example of behaviourist research and how the findings have been applied to human behaviour. Explain whether you think that such a generalisation is reasonable.

Progress exercise

Arguments against the behaviourist approach

There is no doubt that behaviourist explanations are of considerable relevance to understanding human behaviour but they do not explain all behaviour. Radical behaviourism – the view that one can explain all behaviour in terms of conditioning – is a view with very few current supporters. More importantly there are many psychologists who would argue that conditioning can never be a complete explanation of any behaviour. Human behaviour is always affected by a host of factors, only some of which influence animals, such as social context, emotion and cognitive factors. If such factors do influence animal behaviour it would not necessarily result in the same outcomes.

Generalising from animal physiology to human physiology

Behaviourists are concerned with human *behaviour* (not surprisingly) but another important area of psychological research concerns how our physiology works, that is how the body systems work. Human physiology is similar to that of animals in many ways and so, one can argue, it makes sense to conduct invasive procedures on animals in order to make discoveries about human physiology. Examples include the work of Hubel and Wiesel, demonstrating how the visual cortex works. This work was extended to examine the effects of restricted experience on the development of the visual cortex. If this area of the brain is examined in kittens raised in a vertical striped environment (Blakemore and Cooper's study) then it has been found that the cells in the visual cortex that would normally respond to lines of this orientation no longer exist. The brain is altered by experience as long as such experience takes place early in development. Hubel and Wiesel (1970) found that visual deprivation after eight weeks does not have the same effect.

Such research allows us to make sense of human behaviour. Children who are born with a squint (one eye looks in a different direction to the other eye) have difficulty with their binocular vision. Squints can be corrected by performing an operation. However, if this operation is left until after the age of two then vision is permanently damaged (Banks *et al.* 1975). This can be explained in terms of the animal studies. The cells in the visual cortex responsible for making binocular comparisons must have disappeared through lack of experience.

Arguments against physiological comparisons

There are clearly many physiological comparisons that make sense, but there are others that do not. For example, research on sleep deprivation (e.g. Jouvet 1967) and on body rhythms (e.g. Morgan 1995) have both involved stressful procedures with animals (cats and hamsters respectively). Jouvet (1967) used the 'flowerpot technique' to test the consequences of REM deprivation in cats and other animals. He placed an upturned flowerpot in a large tank of water. The cats had to sit on the pots and eventually fell asleep. In NREM sleep they were able to remain sitting up but with loss of muscle tone in REM sleep they slipped into the water and were abruptly awoken. Very soon they woke up as soon as their heads began to nod. In the end the cats died, leading to the conclusion that the lack of REM sleep had been fatal. Morgan conducted research to demonstrate the role of a small organ in the brain (the supra-chiasmatic nucleus, SCN) in the sleep–wake cycle. He used mutant hamsters – hamsters bred to have sleep–wake rhythms of 20 instead of 24 hours. The SCNs from the mutant hamsters were transplanted into a normal hamster who then developed the same abnormal sleep–wake cycle, showing that the SCN governs the sleep–wake cycle.

The only justification for such research is what it might tell us about how human biological rhythms function. However, such rhythms may not be controlled in the same way in humans. It might be, for example, that other organs are involved in human biological rhythms. On the other hand, Green (1994) claims that the basic physiology of the brain and nervous systems of all mammals is essentially the same. Although the human brain might be more highly developed, its similarity to the brains of mammals is far greater than critics of this approach would have us believe.

We should remember, when considering physiological research, that there are many viable alternatives which were not available until more recently: for example, the use of human tissue cultures to test reactions to drugs or biochemical substances. Modern methods of brain scanning permit more accurate identification of brain functions in living brains. Such alternatives mean that we do not have to use animals.

Studying animals to find out about animals

Of course one can justify the benefit of animal research in terms of increased understanding of animal (rather than human) behaviour, and the application of such knowledge to the improvement of animal lives. Certainly ethologists study animals in their natural habitats and provide a wealth of information about the social lives of many animals that increases our knowledge of the natural world.

Commentary

We would question the usefulness of such research to the animals themselves. It might be used to create better zoo environments for captive animals but zoos are for human benefit. Paradoxically evidence about the similarity of animals and humans and the findings of research on animal behaviour might also be used to argue that animals (or at least some animals) are sentient beings who do feel pain in the same way that we do and should not be substitutes for humans in any research.

Ethics: the ethical arguments against using animals

To what extent is research with animals acceptable? Before you make up your mind on this you might like to consider the extent of animal testing in this country (see Box 7.4) or visit some of the websites that put very strong cases either for or against (see the websites at end of chapter).

Pain and distress

It is not simply a case of saying 'we should not be cruel' as no researcher would set out to be deliberately cruel. No one would dispute that research should not involve unnecessary pain or distress to animals. The problems lie in deciding what constitutes unnecessary, and how to assess what pain/distress is experienced by animals.

When trying to decide what research is necessary (or unnecessary) we are stuck in the costs/benefits dilemma discussed in relation to ethics and research with human participants. It is often difficult properly to assess costs before undertaking any study. The calculation of costs and

---

Box 7.4 Animal experiments in the UK

The Home Office publishes data on the use of animals in scientific experiments. There is some controversy about what is and what isn't included in the figures, but they do give a fair estimate of the scale of work in this country involving animals. The data below comes from a review of scientific work carried out during 2002 (Home Office 2003).

Scientific procedures on living animals in Great Britain in 2002 (selected items)

Total number of procedures on animals	2,732,712
Procedures conducted without any anaesthetic	1,634,771
(60 per cent of total)	
Procedures on mice and rats	2,229,915
(82 per cent of total)	
Interference with sight, hearing, smell or taste	16,628
Injection into brain	26,415
Interference with brain	29,039
Procedures deliberately causing psychological distress	9,804
Procedures involving aversive training	7,648
Psychological research	39,642

---

benefits means that one has to decide whose costs and whose benefits. For example, the cost of conducting a study may be measured in terms of distress to participants but can also be measured in terms of the cost of *not* doing the study to those individuals who might have benefited.

Another similar approach to making decisions about the design of animal research was proposed by Bateson (1986). Bateson's decision cube consists of three principles that should jointly determine the acceptability of research:

1. *Quality of the research.* Is the study well designed and carefully thought out?
2. *Degree of animal suffering.* How much pain and distress will be experienced by the animal participants?
3. *Certainty of benefit.* To what extent can we be sure that the findings of research will be useful?

The answers to all three questions can be used to assess whether any study is acceptable in terms of costs and benefits.

Do animals have feelings?

One of the questions in Bateson's decision cube requires an assessment of suffering. How do we assess pain in animals who cannot tell us what they are feeling? Researchers have increasingly found new ways to assess the experience of pain. For example, Sneddon *et al.* (2003) investigated the extent to which fish feel pain. They injected rainbow trout with bee venom and found that they started rocking from side to side, their breathing rate went up and they rubbed their lips on the tank walls. This study raises a key ethical issue. If you argue that it is wrong to inflict pain on an animal then in order to show the animal actually feels pain you have to inflict pain on it. There is also a problem of interpretation in that we cannot say that the fish *feels pain* just because it responds to the noxious stimulus.

We still end up with the question: where do you draw the line? According to Singer (discussed below) the line should be drawn between all sentient beings and all insentient things. However, many animals such as fish, shrimp and clams may be capable of experiencing pain (and therefore shouldn't be used as research subjects). Yet it is also true that they lack most other psychological capacities of higher animals. Do we use the concept of 'psychological capacities' to help us draw the line? What about the fact that fishes actually do form deep lasting relationships when permitted to do so? Can we know a non-human's degree of self-awareness or calculate how richly they experience life? Also if sentience and worthiness depend on specific cognitive abilities, where then is the status of brain-damaged patients who have lost such abilities? Finally one might argue that fishes are actually worthier than most humans, who needlessly cause much suffering and death.

Speciesism

Singer (1975) was one of the first to use the concept of **speciesism**, an 'ism' similar to racism or sexism. Speciesism refers to the 'human intolerance or discrimination on the basis of species, especially as manifested by cruelty to or exploitation of animals'. It has been suggested that the reason that research with animals is acceptable is because they are inferior to humans. Therefore, if we need to conduct research which is harmful in some way then we should do it on animals rather than humans.

The anti-speciesist argument claims that such attitudes are no different to those held in the nineteenth century that black people or women were inferior and therefore not deserving of the same rights. To be biased against individuals because of their membership of a particular species is to be speciesist, which is equivalent to being racist or sexist.

Gray's response to speciesism

Gray (1991) offered two lines of counter-argument to Singer's speciesism. First he made a distinction between moral and ethical arguments. He agreed that it is *ethically* wrong to inflict pain unnecessarily on any species. However, *moral* choices are different. He uses the example of a mother faced with the choice of having to save two small children from a fire. If one of the children is her own, Gray argues, ethically she should display no preference, but most people would find it morally acceptable that she should choose her own child.

Gray's second counter-argument is developed from this example of the mother and child. It is natural (and thus morally acceptable) for a mother to favour her own child. This makes evolutionary sense (any individual should favour their close relatives above others). The same principle can be extended to favouring one's own species over other species. This is a behaviour that is naturally selected. We owe a special duty to our kin and to our own species. As a further example Gray asks what you might do if you saw two creatures fighting and you have a gun if: (a) one is your son and the other is a stranger; (b) both are strangers; (c) one is your son and the other is a lion; (d) one is a stranger and the other is a lion. Obviously in situations (a) and (c) people would save their son. In situation (c), Gray claims that most of people would shoot the lion because they would regard it morally repugnant to shoot the stranger. The reason is that we have a special duty of care to other human beings just because they are humans. Although common sense suggests that we can give a stranger but not a lion a slap, therefore choices are probably constrained by factors other than the moral imperative.

Singer's reply

Singer (1991) claims that Gray's arguments are flawed in many ways. First, there appears to be no general support for the distinction made between ethics and morals, but even if we allow this part of Gray's arguments Singer has more serious objections. The natural selection argument is highly **determinist**, suggesting that human behaviour is driven by genetically programmed instincts that cannot be overridden by reasoned thought. Gray himself suggested that there are some behaviours that are part of our natural heritage which are not morally acceptable, such as the murder of a sexual rival. This means that it is not sufficient to argue that a behaviour is naturally selected and thus acceptable. Furthermore Singer points out that if you open the door to the biological argument there is a lot more that can be 'excused' in human behaviour, such as xenophobia and racism.

Finally, Singer agrees that he too would shoot the lion but this does not make him a speciesist. Singer argues that there is a difference between questions of inflicting pain and questions about taking life. It makes sense to save the life of a human who has the capacity to make plans for the future in preference to an animal who has 'lesser' capacities.

Empty cages

Singer believes that an individual's well-being or life can be sacrificed to the 'greater good'. Although Singer has advocated moral consideration for all sentient beings, he doesn't consider all animals equally entitled to life. In fact, he regards some animals such as fishes as 'replaceable'. Regan (1984) takes a more extreme position. His view is that animals should never be used in research no matter what the benefits and no matter how well their needs are looked after. In his book *Empty Cages* Regan argues that justice does not demand larger, cleaner cages for animal subjects, but empty cages. He argues that human ethics is based on the independent value of the individual and to ignore this individual value is to violate that most basic of human rights: the right of each person to be treated with respect. Why shouldn't this be extended to animals?

Regan further argues that most people would agree that it is wrong to treat weaker human beings, especially those who are lacking in normal human intelligence, as 'renewable resources' or 'commodities'. Our laws don't give less consideration and protection to humans who lack social ties or who do not seem to reflect on their past and future. Regan argues that animals deserve equal justice.

Commentary

It can be argued that the concept of rights only arises as part of a contract between members of society. Individuals are given rights in exchange for responsibilities. Animals have no such responsibilities, cannot reciprocate and therefore it does not seem reasonable to say they have rights.

If you take the absolutist position (see page 9) and follow Singer's approach to speciesism, then clearly you cannot eat animals (unless of course you will also eat people) and you have a problem deciding where the animal world ends. Does it mean you can't take antibiotics because they kill bacteria?

Conclusion

It is important to remember that we are considering the acceptability of *psychological* research. It might be easier to justify medical research, but even then there is the question of whether such research is really valuable. For example, demonstrating that a particular vaccine works on animals may not be generalisable to humans. We should also remember that in the past it was possibly necessary to conduct such research with animals, but today there are many viable alternatives not available then such as human tissue cultures and brain scanning techniques. If the value of and need for medical research is questionable, then the value of and need for psychological research must be even more questionable.

We might then conclude that animal research is difficult to justify because it lacks usefulness and the costs are high. But can we think of one example where this may not have been the case? Harlow's research, which was described earlier, played a key role in changing attitudes to the way we care for children. In the early 1950s people did not think that separation of parents from their children caused much harm. They believed that physical rather than emotional care was more important. Children who spent time in hospital were often visited by their families for only short periods of time because hospitals thought such visits caused more distress than comfort. The research by Harlow provided the kind of evidence that people couldn't argue against. If animals were distressed by such experiences then children must be at least as distressed if not more so.

Summary

Consideration of the use of animals in psychological research must include an appreciation of the way that animals are and have been used, and the value (or not) of such research. It must also recognise the legislation and guidelines that control and advise such research, though these have their drawbacks. These practical considerations may lead us to accept at least some forms of animal research. However, the ethical debate about the rights and wrongs of using animals appears to be moving against psychological research with animals. Singer presents the view that discrimination on the basis of gender, colour or species cannot be justified.

Further reading

Gray, J.A. (1991) On the morality of speciesism, *The Psychologist* 14, 196–8.

Singer, P. (1991) Speciesism, morality and biology: a response to Jeffrey Gray, *The Psychologist* 14, 199–200.

Websites

Psychologists for the ethical treatment of animals

Washoe the chimpanzee

Dian Fossey gorilla site

The argument for animal research <www.rds-online.org.uk>

The argument against animal research

8

Study aids

Improving your essay writing skills

At this point in the book you have acquired the knowledge necessary to tackle the exam itself. Answering exam questions is a skill which this chapter shows you how to improve. Examiners obviously have first-hand knowledge about what goes wrong in exams. For example, candidates frequently do not answer the question which has been set, rather they answer the one that they hoped would come up, or they do not make effective use of the knowledge they have but just 'dump their psychology' on the page and hope the examiner will sort it out for them. A grade C answer usually contains appropriate material but tends to be limited in detail and commentary. To lift such an answer to a grade A or B may require no more than a little more detail, better use of material and coherent organisation. It is important to appreciate that it may not involve writing at any greater length, but might even necessitate the elimination of passages which do not add to the quality of the answer and some elaboration of those which do.

By studying the essays presented in this chapter and the examiner's comments, you can learn how to turn your grade C answer into a grade A. Typically it only involves a few extra marks. Please note that marks given by the examiner in the practice essays should be used as a guide only and are not definitive. They represent the 'raw' marks and are not the same as those given on the examination certificate received ultimately by the candidate because all examining boards are required to use a common standardised system, the Uniform Mark Scale (UMS), which adjusts all raw scores to a single standard across all boards.

In this part of the specification you are also assessed on your ability to be synoptic. Synopticity involves demonstrating a breadth of knowledge and evaluation of a broad range of psychological perspectives and methodologies. In order to maximise your marks you must ensure that you address such issues.

The essays given here are notionally written by an 18-year-old in 40 minutes and marked bearing that in mind. It is important when writing to such a tight time limit that you make every sentence count. Each essay in this chapter is followed by detailed comments about its strengths and weaknesses. The most common problems to watch out for are:

- Failure to answer the question but reproducing a model answer to a similar question which you have pre-learned.
- Not delivering the right balance between description and evaluation/ analysis.
- Writing everything you know about a topic in the hope that something will get credit and the examiner will sort your work out for you. Remember that excellence demands selectivity, so improvements can often be made by removing material which is irrelevant to the question set and elaborating material which is relevant.
- Failing to use your material effectively. It is not enough to place the information on the page, you must also show the examiner that you are using it to make a particular point.

Practice essay 1 AQA(A) style ethics question

> **Describe and evaluate ethical issues that arise in psychological investigations involving human participants. (*30 marks*)**

Starting point: All AQA(A) questions are taken directly from the wording of the specification, as this one has been. The relevant part of the specification says:

Ethical issues involved in psychological investigations using human participants, including the ethics of socially sensitive research. The use of non-human animals in psychological investigations, including constraints on their use and arguments (both ethical and scientific) for and against their use.

So you can expect questions taken straight from this excerpt.

The main pitfalls to avoid are discussing ethical issues in general without making reference to them in specific psychological investigations, or discussing psychological investigations without much mention of the ethical issues. Both pitfalls are quite easy to fall into, especially the second one. Once you start describing a study it is easy to forget the essay question and go off into a general description and evaluation – none of which would be creditworthy. The evaluation in particular must be of the ethical issues and not the investigation itself.

You do need to consider more than one issue and more than one study and might organise your answer along the lines of different ethical issues (and give examples of investigations) or different investigations (and the issues that arise in the study).

Candidate's answer

There have been many psychological studies that have raised ethical issues, most of them are studies in the area of social psychology. Probably the most famous or infamous study was the learning experiment by Milgram. The experiment involved many ethical issues starting with deception at the beginning. Participants were told that the study was about learning but in fact it was about obedience. Participants thought they were giving real electric shocks to another participant but the other participant was in fact a confederate and the shocks weren't real. The participant played the role of a 'teacher' and gave shocks to the learner every time he made a mistake. The shocks were given on a sliding scale which eventually got so strong it would have been fatal if it was real. The participant could hear the confederate screaming and asking them to stop. The 'teacher' asked to stop but was told to continue by the experimenter. 'The experiment requires you to continue.' The situation was very distressing for the participants and many of them were sweating and crying.

The major issue here is deceit which meant that the participants could not give their informed consent. They did give their consent but this didn't count because they didn't know what they were letting themselves in for.

Another issue raised in the study was the right to withdraw. They were told at the start that they could withdraw but when they asked to the experimenter said that it would ruin the experiment if they left.

The participants were very distressed by the experience but they were debriefed afterwards. They were told that they had behaved normally and shouldn't feel bad.

It may seem like there are a lot of ethical issues but we should consider the costs and benefits. Though the costs seem high many of the participants said they were glad to have participated and they didn't seem to suffer long-term harm. If the study had not been done we might not have found out important information. The findings from this study have had big effects. The participants themselves said they would remember to be less mindlessly obedient in future. And the findings helped psychologists to know more about obedience.

Another study that raised a lot of ethical issues was Zimbardo's prison study. This study involved a group of 21 male participants who were assigned the role of a prisoner or guard randomly and asked to spend two weeks in a makeshift prison to see if they would conform to their roles. They conformed all too realistically and the study had to be stopped after 6 days because of the distress experienced by the prisoners. They were made to wash toilets out with their bare hands and woken in the night. They became meek and withdrawn and very depressed. The guards became increasingly violent and appeared to forget their real identity, even volunteering for extra duties. After the experiment finished the guards couldn't believe what they had done and felt very remorseful. The process of wearing a uniform had led to deindividuation.

One issue raised in this study was informed consent. The prisoners were arrested in their own homes and did not realise this was going to happen. They had been told everything else and Zimbardo claimed this had to be done because the police only gave permission right at the end. The prisoners also didn't really give consent because they wouldn't have consented to the degrading treatment they got. This is a problem with informed consent because you can't always predict what will happen so even if you tell participants everything beforehand they cannot truly consent to what will happen.

The more major issue was distress. Again these participants were debriefed about taking part and this debriefing lasted a long time so it may excuse the distress experienced for a short period of time. And Zimbardo did stop the study (though he had to be pushed into doing so by his girlfriend because he was too involved himself to see what was happening).

Zimbardo's study has also been examined from the point of view of costs and benefits. Zimbardo argued that the value of the study was high because it showed that prison violence was due to situational rather than dispositional factors. But others have argued that no changes were made to the prison system so it wasn't important and therefore the benefits don't balance the costs.

Another example of a study where deception took place was Hofling's study of obedience in nurses. This was a field study and in such studies participants can't know about the research beforehand and sometimes it is difficult to debrief them afterwards. So here they didn't know what the study was about or even that they were participating in the study.

There are also socially sensitive issues in research with human participants. There are areas of behaviour which have important social consequences such as research into homosexuality or IQ. The problem is that if you don't do such research because it is socially sensitive then important and useful things may not be discovered. You may not increase people's understanding. If you do do the research it may end up being misused or if the research is flawed (and the conclusions are flawed) people may still print things about it (such as saying there is a homosexuality gene) and then everyone believes it.

Examiner's comments

This is a lengthy answer but does not attract high marks for two main reasons. First, the range of ethical issues and the range of investigations covered is limited. Second, the classic mistake has been made of spending too much time describing the studies and too little time offering commentary.

The AO1 mark is helped by the inclusion of socially sensitive issues at the end though a bit too general (gene research is mentioned).

AO1 = Limited and reasonably detailed = 8 marks.
AO2 = Basic, some elaboration and reasonably effective = 6 marks.
Total = 14 marks out of 30.

Practice essay 2 OCR style ethics question

One of the ethical issues that causes concern in the conduct of psychological investigations is that of deception. It is sometimes argued that the use of deception is an essential part of research and that without some form of deception research would be impossible.

Choose *one* of the core studies listed below and answer the following questions.

- Rosenhan (sane in insane places)
- Milgram (obedience)
- Piliavin, Rodin and Piliavin (subway Samaritans)

(a) Describe how deception was used in your chosen study. (6 marks)
(b) Give *two* reasons supporting the use of deception in your chosen study and *two* reasons against the use of deception in your chosen study. (12 marks)
(c) Suggest *one* way in which your chosen study could have been conducted without the use of deception and say how this might affect the results. (8 marks)

(Total: 26 marks)

OCR December 2003 Question 1 Paper

Starting point: Know your core study. That is the key to success at AS level with OCR. One of the points to bear in mind is that all studies have some ethical dilemmas and it is your job to be able to describe the dilemmas and also to comment on them. Just because we have some concerns about a study it does not mean that it is a rubbish study. You need to be able comment on how important that ethical issue is in the study and whether there is any justification for going against the guideline.

In this question you are asked to do just that. Make a case for and against the ethical conduct of the study you choose to describe.

Candidate's answer

(a) In Milgram's study the participants were told that the shocks they were giving the learners and the 'pain' they were inflicting was real when it was not.

Participants were also under the impression that the learners themselves were participants when they were actually actors.

All screams that participants heard were fake. When a participant shocked up to 450V and they received no further reply from the learners they were deceived to believe that the participant was dead.

Examiner's comments

The candidate makes three decent points about deception in the Milgram study. In fact the whole study is a fake so it is not too difficult to make some point-scoring statements in the answer. The problem many candidates have, however, is that they make general ethical points rather than ones about deception. This candidate has avoided that common error.

Candidate's answer

(b) Arguments as support – It is interesting and important to study the dark side of human nature so we are aware of the kinds of actions humans can commit when they are supposedly justified and even at times when they are not.

The results of the experiment are so significant that the deception is worth it. No psychologists predicted so many participants would go up to the highest voltage. Results give valuable information as to what people can do under the influence of an authority figure. It could explain Nazis under Hitler.

Arguments against – There was a major breach of ethics, people were under the impression that they killed someone causing major psychological harm. Despite being debriefed at the end of the day they had the power to kill someone and they used it. They will never forget this for the rest of their lives.

It is incorrect to deceive someone, and as a result rules were introduced to protect participants. Learners may feel hostility towards the teachers for attempting to kill them and can 'warn' people leading to the teachers' social relationships being affected.

Examiner's comments

Again the candidate has provided a decent answer to the question. They have made two decent points for the use of deception and two decent points against. It is remarkable that we still reference this study to a scene in history that is over 50 years old when there are so many recent examples of people following orders to do harm to others. The answer could have made more of the psychological harm rather than just appearing shocked and amazed. The final point is perhaps a little weak and also a bit muddled.

Candidate's answer

(c) If participants were told that the shocks weren't real it would be assumed that they would obviously go all the way to the maximum voltage because they wouldn't be afflicting any pain on an innocent learner. In which case the study would be pointless.

However if the screams were still present then the participants still may be hesitant as to whether they were in fact giving the shocks. Participants could assume that they were being deceived and the shocks were in actual fact real, which could lead them to stopping at a lower voltage.

If this is the case then participants may be unsure about the experiment being genuine and would stop earlier. The screams could be more intense and the learners could appear that they were being shocked more intensely than they did in the original study, furthermore implying that the shocks were real.

Participants may underestimate how much they would shock as the shocks wouldn't be real.

Examiner's comments

This is a tough question. You are being asked to redesign and improve on Milgram's study. The best answer would probably be to suggest a repeat of the study as a role play. In this case all the participants would be aware of everything and may well be able to act as if it were real. This candidate has made a similar suggestion to this though it could have been thought out and developed better.

Part (a) = 4 marks out of 6.
Part (b) = 7 marks out of 12.
Part (c) = 7 marks out of 8.
Total = 18 marks out of 26.

Practice essay 3

> **Critically consider arguments for the use of non-human animals in psychological research. (30 marks)**

Starting point: Critically consider in 'AQA(A) speak' means 'describe and evaluate'. This question again is taken directly from the AQA(A) specification. The specification mentions arguments for and against the use of non-human animals. This question only asks for the arguments 'for'. You may use the arguments 'against' as the AO2 content of your essay but these will only receive credit if they are used as counter-arguments for each argument 'for' rather than being presented as a stand-alone description of the 'against' arguments.

Note that describing the use of non-human animals in medical research would not be creditworthy.

Candidate's answer

When thinking about the arguments for and against the use of non-human animals (NHA) there are two separate issues: first of all their practical or scientific use, and second the ethical or moral issues around their use.

In terms of scientific arguments, there is the view that it is perfectly legitimate to use NHA in research because they are essentially made of the same building blocks as humans. The nervous systems of mammals are similar and behaviourists would say that the stimulus-response unit is the same in all animals. It just grows to be more complex in humans. So this means that we can conduct research with animals, such as investigating conditioning, and apply this to humans.

The counter-argument to this position is that human behaviour is governed by thinking which is not true for most animals. Therefore human behaviour may be explained differently to animals. For example,

139

something like motivation in humans is affected by how you think about it whereas an animal is driven by instincts. On the other hand some aspects of all animals are the same such as their physiology, though even then biological systems such as sleep work very differently in different animals so it is wrong to generalise from Jouvet's research on cats to human sleep deprivation.

A second scientific argument for using animals is that it is cheaper to use animals in research and also they have shorter life spans so observations can be made of the effects of a treatment over several generations (as was the case in Calhoun's study of rats living in an overcrowded situation). It is also the case that animals can be treated in ways (such as the overcrowding) which you couldn't do to humans. This means you can investigate some behaviours in animals which you could manipulate in humans. This means that at least you have a starting point for understanding human behaviour.

The counter-argument to this is that even if animals are more convenient the ethics of using animals in this way is unacceptable. The main advocate of this position is Tom Regan who says animals shouldn't be used regardless of any benefits for humans. They have rights as well as humans have rights. In the past people thought that women and black people didn't have rights. Our views have changed about women and blacks and Regan thinks that our views about animals will change too. They are sentient beings and we can't treat them as renewable resources.

Singer takes a slightly less radical view and supports the use of animals to a limited extent. He believes that an animal's well-being or life can be sacrificed to the 'greater good'. He doesn't consider that all animals are equally entitled to rights even if they are all sentient. Though he too feels that to distinguish non-human animals from humans is to commit 'speciesism' which is no better than sexism or racism.

Gray argues against speciesism by saying that it may be *ethically* wrong to inflict pain unnecessarily on any species but *morally* we have a duty first and foremost to our own species. It is natural and adaptive to place humans first. It may be ethically wrong to treat animals in this way but it is less objectionable than using humans.

It can further be argued in favour of the use of animals that their use in research has made important contributions to psychological as well as medical science: for example, looking at the link between stress and illness in Selye's research, and also research on drugs for treating psychological problems.

On the other hand most psychological research is not that important – the benefits often don't outweigh the costs. The argument for the use of animals in medical research is different.

It is possible to develop techniques that are less invasive and painful for animals, which would reduce some of the ethical arguments. This would make animal research more ethical. Russell and Birch propose the three Rs – reduction, replacement and refinement – as ways to make animal research more acceptable.

On the other hand researchers might be more pressed to find alternative methods if they were not allowed to use animals.

Finally we should remember that there are strict laws that govern the use of animals. In the UK the Home Office Act requires that any study using animals has a licence and that the researchers have seriously considered not just the treatment of the animals during research but what happens to them afterwards. Some studies that might not seem to be objectionable may affect the rest of the animal's life, such as a learning experiment where an animal has been taught a new set of behaviours which makes it impossible to return them to their natural habitat. This would be an ethical concern and an argument against the use of animals.

Examiner's comments

This answer starts promisingly with an introductory paragraph which is more than just organisation. The first few paragraphs are very clearly organised, distinguishing the description of the arguments for the use of animals (AO1) from the counter-arguments (AO2).

There is then an extended commentary on the views of Regan, Singer and Gray which are not clearly related to the essay title. It is up to the examiner to decide whether to credit this material as description or commentary/evaluation (AO1 and AO2). Probably the Singer and Gray material can all be seen as AO1, with a touch of AO2!

The final paragraphs are not as clearly detailed/elaborated as the earlier material where good use was made of synoptic material (reference to areas of study across the specification).

This is a competent, well-organised essay but doesn't quite hit the top marks because of the lack of detail in places.

AO1 = Description is substantial/slightly limited = 13 marks.
AO2 = Evaluation is slightly limited/thought and reasonably effective
= 12 marks.
Total = 25 marks out of 30.

Journal articles

> Baumrind, D. (1964) Some thoughts on ethics of research: after reading Milgram's behavioural study of obedience, *American Psychologist* 19, 421–3.

In this article Baumrind makes a strong attack on the Milgram (1963) experiment. She starts by noting the dilemma that research psychologists have:

> Certain problems in psychological research require the experimenter to balance his career and scientific interest against the interests of his prospective subjects. (page 421)

The fact that someone volunteers for the study does not take away the researcher's responsibilities towards them. The subject might well give their motives for taking part as wanting to have a stimulating experience or to acquire knowledge or to make a contribution to science. They may also have some private motives such as wanting an opportunity to be noticed by or to confide in a person with psychological training.

Baumrind comments on the relationship between professional workers and clients and suggests that the relationship between subject and psychology experimenter has some special features which are likely to provoke anxiety. For example, the laboratory is an unfamiliar situation and the rules of behaviour are ambiguous. These conditions are likely to make the subject more obedient and more suggestible. It is therefore not the place to carry out studies on obedience.

Baumrind uses some direct quotes from the Milgram (1963) paper to illustrate the lack of regard she says has been given to the subjects. In particular she objects to the detached and objective manner in which Milgram describes the emotional disturbances experienced by his subjects. For example, Milgram writes:

In a large number of cases the degree of tension [in the subjects] reached extremes that are rarely seen in sociopsychological laboratory studies. Subjects were observed to sweat, tremble, stutter, bite their lips, groan, and dig their fingernails into their flesh. These were characteristic rather than exceptional responses to the experiment. (page 375)

Although Milgram debriefed his subjects and attempted to ease their tensions, Baumrind is not convinced and questions whether people are able to put such dramatic and powerful events behind them very easily, if at all. She suggests that the subjects are likely to be left with a number of issues about the hoax they have taken part in and their response to it.

Baumrind considers the idea that the scientific worth of the study balances out the distress caused to the subjects. She accepts that some harm to subjects is a necessary part of research: for example, testing out new medical procedures because the results could not be achieved in any other way. Social psychology, however, is not in the same game as medicine and is unlikely to produce life-saving results and the quality of the methods and the strength of the conclusions do not justify harming subjects. Milgram sees a connection between his study and the behaviour of people who worked in the Nazi death camps. His suggestion is that ordinary people living ordinary lives are capable of playing a part in destructive and cruel acts. Baumrind dismisses this justification for the study and suggests there are few if any parallels between the behaviour in the study and the behaviour in the death camps.

She finishes her review of the study by considering the effect of this work on the public image of psychology and suggests that it will be damaged because it will be perceived that the subjects were not protected or respected.

Reicher, S. and Haslam, A. (2002) Social psychology, science and surveillance: understanding The Experiment, *Social Psychology Review* 5, 7–17.

In May 2002, the BBC broadcast a series of four one-hour programmes entitled *The Experiment*. The series examined the behaviour of 15 men who had been randomly assigned to roles as guards or prisoners within a purpose-built prison over a nine-day period. The study was designed to examine the social, clinical and organisational consequences of assigning people to low or high status groups over an extended period during which a number of experimental manipulations were attempted.

The manipulations related to the permeability of group boundaries, inter-group relations and the participants' awareness of alternatives to the status quo. The results provided support for social identity theory as predicted, but the study also produced some unexpected outcomes. For example, the guards failed to identify with their high status position in the same way that Zimbardo's prison simulation had found (Haney, Banks and Zimbardo 1973). This failure paved the way for the authority of the guards to be overthrown and for a new and more tyrannical regime to emerge. (For more details on the study see the article by Haslam and Reicher 2003 in *Psychology Review*.)

In this article they consider the role of surveillance in the mock prison and whether it contributed to or detracted from the scientific worth of the study. They argue that the participants were not merely play acting to the camera. They note that the filming of the Zimbardo study would have been much more intrusive because of the size and nature film equipment in 1970. They argue that surveillance is part of human life and we feel we are being monitored even when there are no cameras there.

In this study the participants were aware of being monitored by the television cameras and hence the television audience. They were also aware of being monitored by other members of their own group (prisoners or guards), members of the other groups and also by the experimenters. Reicher and Haslam argue that these other audiences sometimes became more important than the audience created by the cameras.

As well as observing what people did, the experimenters also administered psychometric and physiological measures throughout the study. Reicher and Haslam were able to look at their qualitative and quantitative measures to see how they matched up. For example, they were able to look at how inter-group relations related to the stress of the participants during the study. The conflict that was observed in the guards could also be seen in their scores on a burnout scale. While the prisoners' scores stayed the same between days two and five, the guards' scores went up dramatically. The increase in stress was also shown in the physiological measure of cortisol in the saliva. The fact that people (a) acted in a stressed way, (b) indicated on self-report measures that they were stressed and (c) showed physiological changes associated with stress, suggests that the participants were not just playing at stress.

They comment on the conclusions that can be drawn from this and similar studies. They argue that the scientific merit of the study does not come from the generalisations that are made about everyday life, but from the specific hypotheses that were tested during the study:

> It is wrong to see *The Experiment* as a simulation study whose goal was to reproduce the conditions of a real prison. Rather, the study employed elements of a prison and other institutions (an office, a school, a barracks) in order to create a context of group inequality. (page 11)

In their paper, Reicher and Haslam argue that surveillance does not undermine the scientific status of psychological studies and they suggest that psychology could fruitfully spend more time in looking at the science of surveillance.

Glossary

absolute morals The view that some things are simply right or wrong, there is no relative position. For example, murder is wrong no matter what the circumstances are.

behaviourist The view that all behaviour can be explained in terms of learning theory (classical and operant conditioning), referring only to the behaviours themselves rather than any internal mechanisms in order to explain behaviour.

code of conduct A set of principles or guidelines established to guide the behaviour of a group of people, such as doctors or psychologists. Such principles are not laws and transgressions are punished by being disbarred from a professional group.

cognitive development The cognitive (mental) changes that take place as a person grows older, such as changes in memory, perceptual or intellectual abilities.

confederate A colleague of the experimenter who pretends to be a participant during an experiment but is in fact simply following instructions.

debrief A post-research interview designed to inform the participant of the true nature of the study and to restore them to the same state they were in at the start of the experiment. It may also be used to gain useful feedback about the procedures in the study. Debriefing is not an *ethical issue*, it is a means of dealing with ethical issues.

demand characteristics   Features of an experiment that a participant unconsciously responds to when searching for clues about how to behave.

dependent variable (DV)   A measurable outcome of the action of the independent variable in an experiment.

determinist   An argument or theory which proposes that behaviour is established by factors other than one's own will.

disclosed observations   Observing people with their knowledge, which may alter the way they behave.

ecological validity   A form of *external* validity, concerning the ability to *generalise* a research effect beyond the particular setting in which it is demonstrated to other settings.

ethical issues   An ethical issue arises in research where there are conflicts between the research goals and participant's rights.

ethnocentrism   Believing that one's own ingroup (e.g. religious group, nation, gender) is superior to other cultures.

experimenter bias   The effect of an experimenter's expectations, communicated unconsciously, on a participant's behaviour.

imposed etic   A technique or theory that is developed in one culture and then used to study the behaviour of people in other cultures.

independent variable (IV)   Some event that is directly manipulated by an experimenter in order to test its effect on another variable (the dependent variable).

informed consent   An ethical issue and guideline in psychological research whereby participants must be given comprehensive information concerning the nature and purpose of the research and their role in it, in order that they can make an informed decision about whether to participate.

moral   Rules about right and wrong to guide our behaviour based on socially agreed principles. Ethics are a moral framework that is applied to a narrow group of people such as doctors or psychologists.

mundane realism   Refers to how an experiment mirrors the real world.

placebo   A condition that should have no effect on the behaviour being studied, so can be used to separate out the effects of the *independent variable* from any effects caused merely by receiving any treatment.

presumptive consent   A method of dealing with lack of *informed consent* or deception, by asking a group of people who are similar to the participants whether they would agree to take part in a study. If this group of people consents to the procedures in the proposed study it is presumed that the real participants would agree as well.

prior general consent Prospective participants in a research study are asked if they would take part in certain kinds of research, including ones involving deception. If they say yes, they have given their general consent to taking part in such research.

psychoanalytic Freud's explanation of how adult personality develops as a consequence of the interaction between biological (sexual) drives and early experience.

relative morals The view that morals are not absolute but dependent on context so, for example, in some situations stealing is acceptable. The intrinsic 'wrongness' of an act may be overridden by other considerations.

socially sensitive research Research that has direct or indirect social consequences.

speciesism Discrimination on the basis of being a member of a particular species (or not being a member of the human race), similar to racism or sexism where people are discriminated against simply on the basis of race or sex.

undisclosed observations Observing people without their knowledge, for example, using one-way mirrors.

utilitarian approach A theoretical framework for morality where decisions about what is right or wrong are based on the principle of what is useful or practical for the majority of people. Established by weighing costs and benefits for individuals and society.

Notes

1 Introduction

1 'Guardianistas': people who read *The Guardian* and have an irrational belief that they are morally superior to everyone else.
2 The Cold War is the name given to the relationship that developed between the USA and Russia after World War I (1945–1980). It wasn't an actual war but a mutual distrust that dominated international affairs.
3 Spock – closing speech in *Star Trek II: The Wrath of Khan*.
4 Stem cell research involves taking cells from embryos where stem cells are plentiful. These cells are then cultured to produce tissues to be used in treating diseases and injuries.
5 Gamesmanship is the use of dubious (although not technically illegal) methods to win a game, often a sport, such as golf or football.

2 Ethical issues in human research

1 Every time the learner made a mistake the teacher had to administer increasingly strong shocks. If the teacher wished to discontinue, the experimenter (confederate) had a set of instructions to deliver such as saying 'It is absolutely essential that you continue' or 'You have no other choice, you must go on'. Of the 'teachers' 65 per cent went

on to deliver the maximum shock possible – far beyond what was marked 'Danger: severe shock'. Only five participants (12.5 per cent) stopped at 300 volts, the point when the learner first objected.

2 Adolf Eichman was tried in 1961 for his part in transporting Jews, homosexuals and Slavs, among others, to the Nazi concentration camps of World War II (1939–45). His famous defence was that he was just obeying orders. This was not accepted as a sufficient excuse and he was found guilty and hanged.

3 Ethical principles and guidelines

1 The aim of this study was to see if people who experienced significant loss in childhood or adolescence were more likely to fear personal death. This was assessed by asking participants to fill in a scale measuring fear of death.

4 Ethical issues in different kinds of research

1 *Candid Camera* was the name of a TV programme where people were photographed unawares, in amusing and often embarrassing situations.

2 There is some debate about whether studies of such natural variables are actually natural experiments, or are more properly 'difference studies'. Coolican (2004) suggests that in a 'true' natural experiment the independent variable must be something that has been altered rather than an enduring psychological trait such as gender.

3 Zimbardo claimed that permission for the home arrests was only given just before the study took place and therefore there wasn't time to inform participants of this.

4 Clarification: The authors would like to point out that the Banyard and Flanagan Magic Elixir of Life™ is a fictional product and they are not in the business of selling dodgy remedies, just dodgy books.

5 Socially sensitive research

1 Race science: the term race science commonly refers to the various attempts to cover racist ideas with a gloss of scientific respectability. The science is invariably poor and the conclusions are still racist.

6 Psychology in practice

1 Some estimates put it as high as 5,000,000 million dead.
2 This is not meant to be a history lesson, but it is important to have a little context so we can try and understand why people did the things they did.
3 See also the section in Chapter 3 on talking to the media.
4 An example of the level of psychiatric diagnosis can be seen in the figures for medication prescribed in the UK. In 2003, doctors made out 27,700,000 prescriptions for antidepressants. That's an awful lot of pills (www.publications.parliament.uk/pa/cm200405/cmhansrd/cm041221/text/41221w42.htm).

7 Psychological research with non-human animals

1 We use the term 'non-human animals' because the term 'animals' can also include people. This is very clumsy, however, and for the rest of the chapter we will refer to animals.
2 You'll also have to stop eating them (ed.).

References

Ainsworth, M.D.S., Bell, S.M. and Stayton, D.J. (1974) Infant/mother attachment and social development as a product of reciprocal responsiveness to signals, in M.P.M. Richards (ed.) *The Integration of the Child into a Social World*, Cambridge: Cambridge University Press.

APA (2001) Research ethics: comments submitted by APA. Available <www.apa.org/science/comment_nbac-01.html> (accessed 16 June 2005).

APA (2002) <www.apa.org/pi/multiculturalguidelines/> (accessed June 2005).

APS (2001) *William James Fellow Award*. Available <www.psychologicalscience.org/awards/james/citations/loftus.html> (accessed 16 June 2005).

Banks, M.S., Aslin, R.N. and Weiskopf, S. (1975) Sensitive period for the development of human binocular vision, *Science* 190, 675–7.

Banyard, P. (1994) Student practical work: ethical problems for teachers at GCSE and GCE A level, *Psychology Teaching Review* 3(1), 33–40.

Banyard, P. and Hunt, N. (2000) Reporting research: something missing? *The Psychologist* 13(2), 68–71.

Banyard, P. and Shevlin, M. (2000) *Responses of football fans to relegation of their team from the English Premier League: Post-traumatic stress?* Paper presented at the Northern Ireland branch of the British Psychological Society, Carrigart, Ireland.

Baron, R.A. and Byrne, D. (1991) *Social Psychology: Understanding Human Interactions*, 6th edn, Boston: Allyn and Bacon.

Bateson, P. (1986) When to experiment on animals, *New Scientist* 109, 30–32.

Baumrind, D. (1975) Metaethical and normative considerations governing the treatment of human subjects in behavioural sciences, in E.C. Kennedy (ed.) *Human Rights and Psychological Research: A Debate on Psychology and Ethics*, New York: Thomas Crowell.

Bentall, R.P. (1992) A proposal to classify happiness as a psychiatric disorder, *Journal of Medical Ethics* 18(2), 94–8.

Bettelheim, B. (1965) *Love Is Not Enough*, New York: Collier-Macmillan.

Bickman, L. (1974) Clothes make the person, *Psychology Today* 8(4), 48–51.

Blakemore, C. and Cooper, G.F. (1970) Development of the brain depends on the visual environment, *Nature* 228, 477–8.

Bouhoutsos, J.C., Goodchilds, J.D. and Huddy, L. (1986) Media psychology: an empirical study of radio call-in psychology programs, *Professional Psychology: Research and Practice* 17(5), 408–14.

British Psychological Society (BPS) (2000) *Code of Conduct, Ethical Principles and Guidelines*, Leicester: BPS.

Brownell, K.D. and Foreyt, J. (1986) *Handbook of Eating Disorders: Physiology, Psychology and the Treatment of Obesity, Anorexia and Bulimia*, London: HarperCollins.

Canter, D. and Breakwell, G. (1986) Psychologists and 'the media', *Bulletin of the British Psychological Society* 39, 281–6.

Ceci, S.J., Peters, D. and Plotkin, J. (1985) Human subjects review, personal values and the regulation of social science research, *American Psychologist* 40, 994–1002.

Channel 4 (2003) *Inside the Mind of Paul Gascoigne*. Available <www.channel4.com/health/microsites/P/paul_gascoigne/index.html> (accessed June 2005).

Charlton, T., Gunter, B. and Hannan, A. (eds) (2000) *Broadcast Television Effects in a Remote Community*, Hillsdale, NJ: Lawrence Erlbaum Associates Inc.

Christiansen, L. (1988) Deception in psychological research: when is its use justified?, *Personality and Social Psychology Bulletin* 14, 664–75.

Clarke-Carter, D. (1997) *Doing Quantitative Psychological Research*. Hove, UK: Psychology Press.

Colby, A. and Kohlberg, L. (1987) *The Measurement of Moral Judgement. Volume I: Theoretical Formulations and Research Validation. Volume II: Standard Issue Scoring Manual*. Cambridge: Cambridge University Press.

Colman, A.M. (1987) *Facts, Fallacies and Frauds in Psychology*, London: Unwin Hyman.

Coolican, H. (2004) *Research Methods and Statistics in Psychology*, 4th edn, London: Hodder.

Corkin, S.M. (1984) Lasting consequences of bilateral medial temporal lobectomy: clinical course and experimental findings in HM, *Seminars in Neurology* 4, 249–59.

Daeg de Mott, D.K. (2001) *Ethics*, Gale Encyclopedia of Psychology. Available <www.findarticles.com/p/articles/mi_g2699/is_0004/ai_2699000457> (accessed June 2005).

Deaux, K. (1984) From individual difference to social categories: analysis of a decade's research on gender, *American Psychologist* 39, 105–16.

digitalspy. (2003) *Psych Out For Mel*. Available <http://bigbrother.digitalspy.co.uk/article/ds419.html> (accessed June 2005).

Dineen, T. (1999) *Manufacturing Victims: What the Psychology Industry Is Doing to People*. London: Constable and Robinson.

Dunayer, J. (2002) Animal equality. Available <www.upc-online.org/thinking/animal_equality.html> (accessed May 2004).

Edwards, R. (1993) An education in interviewing: placing the researcher and the research, in R. Lee and C. Renzetti (eds) *Researching Sensitive Topics*, pp. 181–96, London: Sage.

Erikson, E.H. (1964) *Insight and Responsibility*, New York: Norton.

Euronet (1998) <www.euronet.nl/~rembert/echelon/202024.htm> (accessed May 2004).

Eysenck, H.J. (1991) *Smoking, Personality and Stress*, New York: Springer-Verlag.

Festinger, L., Riecken, H.W. and Schachter, S. (1956) *When Prophecy Fails*, Minneapolis: University of Minneapolis Press.

Florian, V. and Mikulincer, M. (1998) Symbolic immortality and the management of the terror of death – the moderating role of attachment style, *Journal of Personality and Social Psychology* 74, 725–34.

Frank, E. (1983) Psychology at six: presenting psychological information to a mass audience in a news format, *Clinical Psychologist* 36(2), 35–37.

Freud, S. (1973) *The New Introductory Lectures on Psychoanalysis*, Harmondsworth: Penguin, first published 1933.

Fukuyama, F. (2001) *Natural Rights and Human History*. The National Interest. Available <www.findarticles.com/p/articles/mi_m2751/is_2001_Summer/ai_76560812> (accessed June 2005).

Gamson, W.B., Fireman, B, and Rytina, S. (1982) *Encounters with Unjust Authority*, Homewood, IL: Dorsey Press.

Gardner, B.T. and Gardner, R.A. (1969) Teaching sign language to a chimpanzee, *Science* 165, 664–72.

Gray, J.A. (1991) On the morality of speciesism, *The Psychologist* 14, 196–8.

Green, S. (1994) *Principles of Biopsychology*, Hove, UK: Lawrence Erlbaum Associates Ltd.

Greenberg, M. (1967) Role-playing: an alternative to deception?, *Journal of Personality and Social Psychology* 7, 152–7.

Guardian (2003) *Kick 'em while they're down*. The Guardian. Available <http://media.guardian.co.uk/broadcast/comment/0,7493,996086,00.html> (accessed 11 July 2003).

Guardian (2004) Tensions that start in playground. The Guardian. Available <www.guardian.co.uk/uk_news/story/0,3604,1183235,00.html> (accessed June 2005).

Haney, C., Banks, C. and Zimbardo, P. (1973) A study of prisoners and guards in a simulated prison, *Naval Research Review* 30, 4–17.

Harlow, H.F. (1959) Love in infant monkeys, *Scientific American* 200(6), 68–74.

Haslam, A. and Reicher, S. (2003) A tale of two prison experiments: beyond a role-based explanation of tyranny, *Psychology Review* 9(4), 2–6.

Heider, F. (1958) *The Psychology of Interpersonal Relations*, New York: Wiley.

Hewstone, M., Stroebe, W., Codol, J.P. and Stephenson, G. (1988) *Introduction to Social Psychology: A European Perspective*, Oxford: Blackwell.

Home Office (2003) *Statistics of Scientific Procedures on Living Animals Great Britian 2002*, London: The Stationery Office.

House of Lords (2002) *Select Committee on Animals in Scientific Procedures*. <www.parliament.the-stationery-office.co.uk/pa/ld200102/ldselect/ldanimal/150/15003.htm> (accessed June 2005).

Hubel, D.H. and Wiesel, T.N. (1970) The period of susceptibility to the physiological effects of unilateral eye closure in kittens, *Journal of Physiology* 206, 419–36.

Hubel, D.H.,Wiesel, T.N. and LeVay, S. (1977) Plasticity of ocular dominance columns in monkey striate cortex, *Philosophical Transactions of the Royal Society of London Series B* 278, 377–409.

Humphreys, L. (1970) *Tearoom Trade: A Study of Homosexual Encounters in Public Places*, Chicago: Aldine.

Jensen, A.R. (1969) How much can we boost IQ and scholastic achievement?, *Harvard Educational Review* 39, 1–123.

Jones, J.H. (1993) *Bad Blood: The Tuskegee Syphilis Experiment*, New York: Free Press

Jones, J. M. (1991) Psychological models of race: what have they been and what should they be?, in J. D. Goodchilds (ed.) *Psychological Perspectives on Human Diversity in America*, pp. 3–45, Washington: American Psychological Association.

Jouvet, M. (1967) Mechanisms of the states of sleep: a neuropharmological approach, *Research Publications of the Association for the Research in Nervous and Mental Disorders* 45, 86–126.

Joynson, R.B. (1989) *The Burt Affair*, London: Routledge.

Kamin, L. (1974) *The Science and Politics of IQ*, Harmondsworth: Penguin.

Katz, J. (1972) *Experimentation with Human Beings*, New York: Russell Sage Foundation.

Keith-Spiegel, P. and Koocher, G. (1985) *Ethics in Psychology: Professional Standards and Cases*, New York: Random House.

Kimmel, A.J. (1996) *Ethical Issues in Behavioural Research*, Oxford: Blackwell.

Kinsey, A.C. *et al.* (1948) *Sexual Behaviour in the Human Male*, Philadelpia: Saunders.

Kirk, S. and Kutchins, H. (2000) Revolution – in rhetoric, *Openmind* 104, 8–9.

Kitzinger, C. (1998) Challenging gender biases: feminist psychology at work, *Psychology Review* 4, 18–20.

Kline, P. (1991) *Intelligence: The Psychometric View*, London: Routledge.

Kohlberg, L. (1978) Revisions in the theory and practice of moral development, *Directions for Child Development* 2, 83–8.

Lee, R.M. (1993) *Doing Research on Sensitive Topics*, London: Sage.

Lee, R.M. and Renzetti, C.M. (1993) The problems of researching sensitive topics, in R. M. Lee and C. M. Renzetti (eds) *Researching Sensitive Topics*, Newbury Park: Sage.

Levin, P. and Arluke, A. (1985) An exploratory analysis of sex differences in gossip, *Sex Roles* 12, 281–6.

LeVine, R.A. and Campbell, D.T. (1972) *Ethnocentrism: Theories of Conflict, Ethnic Attitudes and Group Behaviour*, New York: Wiley.

Liebling, H. and Shah, S. (2001) Researching sensitive topics: investigations of the sexual abuse of women in Uganda and girls in Tanzania, *Law, Social Justice and Global Development (LGD)* <http://elj.warwick.ac.uk/global/issue/2001-1/liebling.html> (accessed 17 January 2005).

Lilly, J.C. (1956) Mental effects of reduction of ordinary levels of physical stimuli on intact healthy persons, *Psychological Research Reports* 5, 1–9.

Loftus, E. (1998) The price of bad memories, *Skeptical Inquirer* 22, 23–4.

Lynn, S.J., Loftus, E., Lilienfeld, S. and Lock, T. (2003) Memory recovery techniques in psychotherapy: problems and pitfalls. Skeptical Inquirer. Available <www.findarticles.com/p/articles/mi_m2843/is_4_27/ai_104733238> (accessed June 2005).

McGuffin, J. (1974) *The Guinea Pigs*. Irish Resistance Books. Available <www.irishresistancebooks.com/guineapigs/guineapigs.htm> (accessed June 2005).

Maccoby, E.E. and Jacklin, C. (1974) *The Psychology of Sex Differences*, Stanford, CA: Stanford University Press.

McCosker, H., Barnard, A. and Gerber, R. (2001) Undertaking sensitive research: issues and strategies for meeting the safety needs of all participants, *Forum: Qualitative Research* 2(1). <www.qualitative-research.net/fqs-texte/1-01/1-01mccoskeretal-e.htm> (accessed 16 June 2005).

Matlin, M.W. (1987) *The Psychology of Women*, London: Holt, Rinehart and Winston.

Milgram, S. (1963) Behavioural study of obedience, *Journal of Abnormal and Social Psychology* 67, 371–8.

Milgram, S. (1974) *Obedience to Authority*, New York: Harper and Row.

Miller, G. (1969) Psychology as a means of promoting human welfare, *American Psychologist* 24, 1063–75.

Moore, H.T. (1922) Further data concerning sex differences, *Journal of Abnormal and Social Psychology* 17, 210–14.

Morgan, E. (1995) Measuring time with a biological clock, *Biological Sciences Review* 7, 2–5.

Nobles, W. (1976) Extended self: rethinking the so-called negro self concept, *Journal of Black Psychology* 2, 15–24.

NYAC (2003) 'Bug chasing' gains more widespread attention. Available <www.nyaidscoalition.org/cgi-bin/iowa/nyac/news/cityhall/407.html> (accessed June 2005).

Ogden, J.A. and Corkin, S. (1991) Memories of HM, in W.C. Abraham, M.C. Corballis and K.G. White (eds) *Memory Mechanisms: A Tribute to G.V. Goddard*, pp. 195–215, Mahwah, NJ: Lawrence Erlbaum Associates Inc.

Olds, J. and Milner, P. (1954) Positive reinforcement produced by electrical stimulation of the septal area and other regions of the rat brain, *Journal of Comparative and Physiological Psychology* 47, 419–28.

Ouseley, H. (2001) *Community Pride not Prejudice*. Making Diversity Work in Bradford, Bradford Race Review, Bradford Council. Available http://www.bradford2020.com/pride/ (accessed June 2005).

Parker, B. and Ulrich, Y. (1990) A protocol of safety: research on abuse of women, *Nursing Research* 39(4), 248–9.

Parkin, A.J. (1996) HM: the medial temporal lobes and memory, in C. Code, C.W. Wallesch, Y. Joanette and A.B. Lecours (eds) *Classic Cases in Neuropsychology*, Hove, UK: Psychology Press.

Pilger, J. (1975) *The Last Day*, London: Mirror Group Books.

Pilger, J. (1989) *Heroes*, London: Pan.

Piliavin, I., Rodin, J. and Piliavin, J. (1969) Good Samaritanism: an underground phenomenon?, *Journal of Personality and Social Psychology* 13, 289–99.

Plous, S. (1996) Attitudes toward the use of animals in psychological research and education: results from a national survey of psychology majors, *Psychological Science* 7, 352–8.

Pope, K. (2001) Sex between therapists and clients, in J. Worell (ed.) *Encyclopedia of Women and Gender: Sex Similarities and Differences and the Impact of Society on Gender*, New York: Academic Press.

Pope, K. and Vetter, V.A. (1991) Prior therapist–patient sexual involvement among patients seen by psychologists, *Psychotherapy* 28(3), 429–38.

Ramsey, S. (2001) Audit further exposes UK's worst serial killer, *The Lancet* 357, 123–4.

Rapoff, M.A. (1980) Suppression of self-injurious behaviour: determining the least restrictive alternative, *Journal of Mental Deficiency Research* 24, 37–42.

Raviv, A., Raviv, A. and Yunovitz, R. (1989) Radio psychology and psychotherapy: comparison of client attitudes and expectations, *Professional Psychology: Research and Practice* 20(2), 67–72.

Regan, T. (1984) *The Case for Animal Rights*, New York: Routledge.

Regan, T. (2004) *Empty Cages: Facing the Truth about Animal Cruelty in America*. Lanham, MD: Rowman and Littlefield.

Renzetti, C.M. and Lee, R.M. (1993) *Researching Sensitive Topics*, London: Sage.

Riesen, A.H. (1956) Effects of early deprivation of photic stimulation, in S. Oster and R. Cook (eds) *The Biosocial Basis of Mental Retardation*, Baltimore: Johns Hopkins University Press.

Rosenzweig, M.R. (ed.) (1992) *International Psychological Science, Progress, Problems, and Prospects*. Washington, DC: American Psychological Association.

Rushton, J. (1990) Race differences, r/K theory and a reply to Flynn, *The Psychologist* 5, 195–8.

Russell, W.M.S. and Birch, R. (1959) *The Principles of Humane Experimental Technique*, London: Methuen.

Rymer, R. (1993) *Genie – Escape from a Silent Childhood*, London: Michael Joseph.

Schachter, S. (1959) *The Psychology of Affiliation*, Stanford, CA: Stanford University Press.

Schulz, F. (2000) The humanist basis for human rights. Humanist. Available <www.findarticles.com.> (accessed June 2005).

Scoville, W.B. and Milner, J. (1957) Loss of recent memory after bilateral hippocampal lesions, *Journal of Neurochemistry* 20(1), 11–21.

Seligman, M.E.P. and Maier, S.F. (1967) Failure to escape tramatic shock, *Journal of Experimental Psychology* 74, 1–9.

Seyfarth, D.M. and Cheyney, D.L. (1980) The ontogeny of vervet monkey alarm calling behaviour: a preliminary report, *Zeitschrift für Tierpsychologie* 54, 37–56.

Shallice, T. (1973) The Ulster depth interrogation techniques and their relation to sensory deprivation research, *Cognitive Psychology* 1, 385–405.

Shelman, E.A. and Lazoritz, S. (1999) Out of the darkness: the story of Mary Ellen Wilson, Baltimore, MD: Dolphin Moon Publishing.

Sherif, M. (1956) Experiments in group conflict, *Scientific American* 195, 54–8.

Shevlin, M., Brunsden, V., Walker, S., Davies, M. and Ramkalawan, T. (1997) Death of Diana, Princess of Wales, *British Medical Journal* 315, 1467–8.

Sieber, J. E. (1995) *Planning Ethically Responsible Research: A Guide for Students and Internal Review Boards*, London: Sage.

Sieber, J. (2005) Socially sensitive research, *Psychology Review* 11(1), 6–9.

Sieber, J.E. and Stanley, B. (1988) Ethical and professional dimensions of socially sensitive research, *American Psychologist* 43, 49–55.

Singer, P. (1975) *Animal Liberation*, New York: Avon.

Singer, P. (1991) Speciesism, morality and biology: a response to Jeffrey Gray, *The Psychologist* 14, 199–200.

Skinner, B.F. (1960) Pigeons in a pelican, *American Psychologist* 15, 28–37.

Sloboda, J. (2001) Psychologists and public policy: ethical dilemmas. Paper presented at the European School Psychologists for Research, Information and Exchange (ESPRIE), London, 22 November.

Sloboda, J. and Coleman, P. (2001) Taking a stand, *The Psychologist* 13(11), 550–51.

Smith, P.B. and Bond, M.H. (1993) *Social Psychology Across Cultures*, Hemel Hempstead: Harvester Wheatsheaf.

Smith, S. and Lewty, W. (1959) Perceptual isolation using a silent room, *The Lancet* 12, 342–5.

Sneddon, L.U., Braithwaite, V.A. and Gentle, M.J. (2003) Do fish have nociceptors: evidence for the evolution of a vertebrate sensory system, *Proceedings of the Royal Society B* June, 1115.

Stein, M.B., Walker, J.R. and Forde, D.R. (1996) Public-speaking fears in a community sample: prevalence, impact on functioning and diagnostic classification, *Archives of General Psychiatry* 53(2), 169–74.

Steinberg, M. and Schnall, M. (2001) *The Stranger in the Mirror*, New York: Cliff Street Books.

Summerfield, D. (2000) War and mental health: a brief overview, *British Medical Journal* 321, 232–5.

SunSpot.net (2003) Sea lions, dolphins aid U.S. troops: aquatic mammals trained to mark marine mines, disable enemy divers. Baltimoresun.com. Available <http://www.sunspot.net/news/nationworld/iraq/bal-te.dolphins26mar26,0,1891645.story?coll=bal-home-headlines> (accessed June 2005).

Tajfel, H. (1970) Experiments in intergroup discrimination, *Scientific American* 223, 96–102.

Thigpen, C. and Cleckley, H. (1954) A case of multiple personality, *Journal of Abnormal and Social Psychology* 49, 135–51.

Tunnicliff, P.L. (1998) Ethics of experimentation: a replication without deception. <www.faculty.sfasu.edu/gford/EthicsofExperimentation.htm> (accessed July 2005).

Watson, P. (1980) *War on the Mind*, Harmondsworth: Pelican.

Weisstein, N. (1992) Psychology constructs the female, or the fantasy life of the male psychologist (with some attention to the fantasies of his friends the male biologist and the male anthropologist), in J. S. Bohan (ed.) *Seldom Seen, Rarely Heard: Women's Place in Psychology*, pp. 61–78, Boulder, CO: Westview.

Westin, A.F. (1968) *Privacy and Freedom*, New York: Atheneum.

Williams, J. (1987) *Psychology of Women: Behavior in a Biosocial Context*, 3rd edn, New York: Norton.

Windle, C. and Vallance, T. (1964) The future of military psychology and paramilitary psychology, *American Psychologist* 19(2), 119–29.

Woolley, H.T. (1910) Psychological literature: a review of the recent literature on the psychology of sex, *Psychological Bulletin* 7, 335–42.

World Health Organization (WHO) (2001) *Mental Health: New Understanding, New Hope*, Geneva: World Health Organization.

World Health Organization (WHO) (2004) *The International*

Statistical Classification of Diseases and Related Health Problems. World Health Organization. Available <www.who.int/whosis/icd10/> (accessed 2004).

Zimbardo, P.G. (1989) *Quiet Rage: The Stanford Prison video*, Stanford, CA: Stanford University.

Zubek, J.P. (1969) *Sensory Deprivation: Fifteen Years of Research*, New York: Appleton-Century-Croft.

Index